Other Books by this Author

I Want To Be Me But I Don't Know Who I Am
A Guidebook for Teens and Young Adults

Series: I Want to Be Me; (Volume 1)

© 2017

I Want To Be Me. Introduction to the Guidebook and Workbook

80-page gift to mailing list subscribers

Includes introductory material and a chapter from each book

© 2020

Soon to be Published
I Want To Be Me App

App helps users measure progress in Identity and Behavior
and helps users build Decision Trees

I Want To Be Me Web Course for Teens and Young Adults

Course will cover the book in 8 modules

Please visit www.Iwanttobeme.org for news and blogs; sign up for announcements of sales
and new materials that become available.

I Want To Be Me

WORKBOOK

Pre-Teens · Teens · Young Adults

Madeleine Boskovitz, Ph.D.

CORYMARC PUBLISHING

Author's Note to the Reader: This book offers advice, education, and encouragement to teens and young adults. It does not offer or replace professional psychological or therapeutic treatment, nor is it meant to replace other professional interventions.

CorymarC Publishing, Philadelphia, PA

Published in the United States by CorymarC Publishing, Philadelphia, PA

ISBN: 978-0-9987786-2-4

Author Name: Madeleine Boskovitz

Title: I Want To Be Me Workbook: Pre-Teens, Teens, Young Adults.

Series: I WANT TO BE ME ; (Volume 2)

Interest Age Level: 13-20

Subjects: Self-Actualization, Self-Esteem in Teens; Self-Esteem in Young Adults; Teen Handbook; Self-Confidence in Teens; Self-Confidence in Young Adults; Self-Management in Teens; Self-Management in Young Adults; Self-Help for Teens; Self-Help for Young Adults; Self-Care for Teens; Self-Care for Young Adults; Resilience;, Development of Autonomy in Teens; Development of Autonomy in Young Adults.

Cover Font: © Paratype

Cover Photos and Cameos: © Adobe Stock Photos

Cover design and chapter headers: RC Creative, Marc Sawaya ©2019

This workbook is dedicated to all teens and young adults who are engaged in the challenging work of becoming adults.

Preface

This I WANT TO BE ME WORKBOOK (for) Pre-Teens, Teens, and Young Adults, and the I WANT TO BE ME BUT I DON'T KNOW WHO I AM, A Guidebook for Teens and Young Adults, are largely based on the pioneering work of French psychiatrist and pediatrician, Francoise Dolto, MD, whose prolific writings I had the good fortune to study before I became a psychologist and a parent. It has guided my approach to life with my children and to the clinical work that I perform. I also had the good fortune of meeting Dr. Francoise Dolto several times and am still in contact with her daughter, Dr. Catherine Dolto, a pediatrician who has written many books about health for young children, also following her mother's approach.

Dr. Francoise Dolto advocated tirelessly for respect for children. This respect was initiated by listening to children even before they could talk and by speaking their truth to them. Being told their truth is essential for healthy survival, even for infants. Abandoned infants, seen by Dr. Dolto in a hospital ward, were refusing to live but, as she talked to them about what was happening to them, as she acknowledged the truth of their situation, the infants looked at peace and began to thrive. In France, where her work was popular and well-known, there is said to be a "before" and an "after" Francoise Dolto, due to her major influence on child raising.

This work is addressed directly to all teens and young adults, in an easy, kind, and respectful language. It focuses on those who need it the most, because their situation is often difficult and confusing. It shows them the basics of self-care and identity building. It shows them that they have many choices and can make the choices that will help them grow healthy, resilient, and successful, however they define success. There is no success too small or too large.

While Dr. Dolto (1908-1988) has written many volumes, most of which have been translated into many languages, her work is largely unknown in the United States. It is my sincere hope to make her valuable wisdom available here, as well.

Table of Contents

Introduction

The I WANT TO BE ME WORKBOOK. Pre-Teens.Teens.Young Adults is a companion volume to the previously published guidebook: I WANT TO BE ME BUT I DON'T KNOW WHO I AM. A Guidebook for Teens and Young Adults.

The WORKBOOK elaborates on concepts taught in the guidebook and offers readers the opportunity to apply them to their specific life experience. It gives direction and offers the support needed to grow through the teen and young adult years.

Milestones for pre-teens have been included to ensure that the teen reader is ready to engage in the developmental tasks of adolescence: managing emotions and behavior, gradually separating from parents and caretakers, developing autonomy and responsibility, and ultimately making choices that protect their dreams and goals.

Those who read the Guidebook and work through the Workbook's exercises can expect to feel empowered to manage their lives in a positive and constructive manner even when faced with major obstacles.

Throughout this Workbook, the reader is provided with tables and worksheets to fill in. In addition, copies of those forms and journal pages are available online.

Copies of the tables and worksheets are available at www.iwanttobeme.org

A link to a video explaining Decision Tree building is also available

Access Code: bisdt2017

Watch for the new I WANT TO BE ME APP coming soon!

The App will help the reader keep track of personal progress on the Scales and practice building Decision Trees

CHAPTER 1

Dr. B Holds Up The Mirror

Introduction

Before focusing on you, we will review important concepts from the first chapter in the guidebook. You need to understand these if you want to benefit from this work.

First, you are going to start looking at yourself, identify some of your parts. First comes what we call demographic information—simple facts about you and your life. You can add things about your life, such as where you live, today's date, and other facts as well.

Next, you'll take a good look at yourself, how you were in the past, how you are now, and how you want to be in the future. For example, many teens say they were happier when they were kids (before becoming teens), and they want to be happier in the future.

You'll also identify your past and present behaviors, and what you want them to be. Remember, this is all private, so you can be honest with yourself. If you are honest with yourself, it will be much more valuable to you.

Then, you will think about your dreams. Don't be embarrassed: no dream is "unrealistic." Every dream is valuable and needs to be acknowledged and honored (even if it seems impossible). You'll identify goals to reach on the way to succeeding. You may not know the steps and goals. This is a good time to think about them anyway.

Finally, you'll encounter the Decision Trees. These may seem a bit scary and too difficult at first, but you'll see that they really are not. They help you think about your choices, and "predict the future." This is a great skill that will help you throughout your life.

Enjoy discovering yourself!

Part 1. Understanding Important Concepts

These are the most important concepts in the Guidebook. For each of the terms below, I entered the definition from the Guidebook. How does each term apply to you ?

Identity: The person you are, the way others see you. How do you see yourself?

_____

_____

_____

Awareness: Knowing who you are, what you do, what you want for yourself. Are you aware?

_____

_____

_____

Privacy: Keeping things to yourself; this is essential for honesty. Can you keep things private?

_____

_____

_____

Honesty: acknowledging your truth; this is needed for this work to have value. Can you be honest?

_____

_____

_____

True voice: Listen to the one voice that wants the best for you. Can you hear yours?

_____

_____

_____

Dreams: Wishes you have for yourself. Do you have dreams?

_____

_____

_____

<u>Self-soothing</u>: taking care of yourself when you are hurt or angry. What do you do?

_____

_____

_____

<u>Becoming your own parent</u>: The best parent that looks out for you. Can you do that for yourself?

_____

_____

_____

<u>Good choices</u>: Make choices that fit your <u>goals</u>. How do you make choices?

_____

_____

_____

<u>Being Empowered</u>: Feeling in charge of your life. Do you feel that way at times?

_____

_____

_____

<u>Resilient</u>: Managing to stay on course despite obstacles. Can you do that sometimes?

_____

_____

_____

<u>Courage</u>: Doing things even when one is scared to do them. Can you find your courage?

_____

_____

_____

Part 2. Demographics: Your Personal Information

Name: _____ Age: _____

Sex: Male Female   Gender Identity: Male Female Non-Binary

Sexual Orientation: _____

Height: _____ Weight: _____ Hair color: _____ Eye color: _____

Ethnic Identity:_____ Birth Place: _____

Father's Ethnic Identity: _____ Mother's: _____

Living with: Mother Father Stepmother Stepfather Grandmother Grandfather Aunt/Uncle
Foster parent Guardian Other_____

I also live with: Sister(s)   Brother(s)   Half-brother(s)   Half-sister(s)

                    Stepbrother(s)   Stepsister(s)   Cousin(s)   My child(ren)

Pets: Dog   Cat   Bird   Reptile   Fish   Other:

School: _____ Grade: _____

My Favorite subjects: _____

My sports: _____

My other activities: _____

My friends:

Name: _____ Age: _____ Gender: _____

Name: _____ Age: _____ Gender: _____

Name: _____ Age: _____ Gender: _____

Name: _____ Age: _____ Gender: _____

Name: _____ Age: _____ Gender: _____

Name: _____ Age: _____ Gender: _____

Part 3. The Identity Scale – Knowing Your Qualities

Describing your traits or qualities that are not physical is difficult. You know them and they do "show" when others get to know you but it's not so easy to be aware of them and able to name them. However, it is most important to become aware of them and able to identify them by name. Why? Because it is only when you are aware of who you are that you can make the choices that fit you. You will soon see what I mean.

This is your Identity Scale

It is private. Only you can see it. Only you can make changes to it. Of course, you can show it to others if you like, but it is your private scale to do with as you wish.

The Identity Scale has many pairs of opposite qualities. No one is all one or the other but somewhere in between, along the dotted line. It is up to you to decide where you fit on the scale. For each pair, there will be three measurements.

The first marker, P for Past, is to evaluate where you were before you became a teen. Think of yourself before this time and decide where you were on the scale. It is entirely up to you where you place your P; remember, it's your private experience.

Next is T. T is for Today and you can decide where you are every time you check out the Identity Scale. It is important. Was there some movement for you? In which direction? Maybe no movement? Is that what you wanted?

The last marker, F for Future is important. Place it where you would like to be. This way, you can see what you are wishing for yourself, what you are working towards. This button can move. As you go along, you may set different goals for yourself.

When I first did this exercise with teens, they were immediately excited. Being able to have this glimpse at themselves really spoke to them. I hope it is useful for you, too.

Think of the book's cover. It shows teens and young adults searching for who they are, trying to find their direction. This scale is to help you see more clearly who you are, where you are going, and where you want to go.

Some terms are easy to understand; others need explanation. Teens who are ambitious have goals that they want to reach. Discouraged teens have given up on goals for themselves. Excitable teens get frustrated easily. They tend to have a temper. Teens who are independent do things by themselves and make their own decisions. Dependent teens need others to tell them what to do. Jealous teens think others have it better. Secure teens look at themselves and decide what they want for themselves.

I have also left blank spaces for you to add your own pairs of qualities that are important or difficult for you.

The position of each marker will change only if you change it. I do encourage you to change the Today marker as often as you need to show a change. You may also want to change the Future marker as needed. You may even change the Past marker if you remember something different and want to change it. (I recommend that you revisit your Identity and Behavior Scale markers every week). When the new I Want To Be Me App comes out, this will become very easy. (Be sure to check www.iwanttobeme.org).

Example: This is how I would have answered the first question when I was a teen.

Happy...................F.........................T......................P.........................Sad

Feelings are not black and white; they are on a continuum. You can see here that my current feeling is somewhere in the middle between Happy and Sad. When I was younger, I was sadder: there were bad things happening in my home. I, of course, want to be much happier in the future.

Identity Scale

Happy	Sad
Outgoing	Shy
Friendly	Unfriendly
Hopeful	Hopeless
Ambitious	Discouraged
Relaxed	Worried
Cool	Bad temper
Peaceful	Angry
Independent	Dependent
Brave	Fearful
Secure	Insecure
Not Jealous	Jealous
Kind	Mean
Loving	Hating
Truthful	Lying
Respectful	Manipulative
Focused	Scattered

Confident	Insecure
Active	Slow-moving
Honest	Cheating
Caring	Careless
Trusting	Scared
Courageous	Discouraged
Straightforward	Devious

Part 4. The Behavior Scale – Knowing Your Behavior

In the original workshop, I had only the Identity Scale. In this book, I have added the Behavior Scale to help you appraise the choices you make, the behaviors you engage in.

Your choice of behavior is important for your present and for the future you are creating. It is essential to think about these choices and be honest with yourself when using the scale. Remember that no one else will see this. It is your private place. I hope that my holding this mirror up to you will help you see more clearly where you are and, most important, where you want to be. You can get there. The more honest you are, the easier it will be for you as you will be forging a straight path to your goals.

Here again, you will have the three markers, P for Past, T for Today, and F for Future, that you can use to see where you have been, where you are now, and where you want to be. Most important is to move these markers often to show any change in your behavior. Are you going in the direction that you want?

Finally, you have blank spaces to add behaviors that are important or challenging for you.

My example:

Doing Homework P..........................T...F No Homework

When I was little, my mother made me do all my homework. Now I skip some of it if I feel I don't need it. I still do most of it. In the future, I want to be done with homework, of course! But, in real life, we always have "homework," things that need doing.

Behavior Scale

Eating breakfast .... No breakfast

Doing homework .... No homework

Obeying parents .... Disobeying parents

Doing classwork .... no classwork

Being calm in class .... Acting out in class

Obeying teachers .... Disobeying teachers

Managing school behavior .... Getting detention/suspended

Attending school .... Skipping school

Obeying the law .... Having legal troubles

Being honest .... Cheating, Lying/Stealing

Studying for tests .... Blowing off tests

Treating others well .... Bullying others

Eating regular meals .... Skipping meals

Helping at home .... Refusing responsibility

Helping brothers and sisters .... Avoiding helping

Personal cleanliness .... Poor personal care

Being careful .... Engaging in risky behaviors

Being independent .... Joining a gang

Being respectful .... Mocking others

Being sober .... Drinking alcohol

Being drug free .... Using drugs

No tobacco .... Using tobacco

No weed .... Smoking weed

Staying clear .... Selling drugs/pot

15

Part 5. Know Your Dreams, Wishes, and Goals

We all have dreams and wishes. Remember this work is private. You can share it with others if you like but you can also keep it to yourself.

No dream or wish is too big or too small. Be honest with yourself and be brave enough to acknowledge your dreams.

Dream # 1: _____

_____

_____

_____

How could you make this dream happen? Setting goals towards it is a good first step. Start with the smallest first step. You will see that there may well be a path to your dream. It's always worth a try. It's your life.

Goal # 1: _____

_____

_____

_____

Goal # 2: _____

_____

_____

_____

Goal # 3: _____

_____

_____

_____

Dream # 2: _____

_____

_____

_____

How could you make this dream happen? Setting goals towards it is a good first step. Start with the smallest first step. You will see that there may well be a path to your dream. It's always worth a try. It's your life.

Goal # 1: _____

_____

_____

_____

Goal # 2: _____

_____

_____

_____

Goal # 3: _____

_____

_____

_____

Dream # 3: _____

_____

_____

_____

How could you make this dream happen? Setting goals towards it is a good first step. Start with the smallest first step. You will see that there may well be a path to your dream. It's always worth a try. It's your life.

Goal # 1: _____

_____

_____

_____

Goal # 2: _____

_____

_____

_____

Goal # 3: _____

_____

_____

_____

Part 6. A First Look at Decision Trees

First, let me say that they are not as difficult as they look. When you look at the blank decision tree, it seems complicated. But let's look carefully. We start at the first box on the left: the decision to be made. It's a YES/NO choice. You decide YES, then consider what happens next, again a YES/NO result and new choice. Or you decide NO, then consider what happens next, again a YES/NO result and new choice. This just keeps going.

The challenge is to take it one step at a time. Keep the goal in mind but do not jump to the goal or conclusion. The outcome of the goal is always in the last column on the right. We are trying to see how decisions may or may not lead to the desired goal. Learning to look at choices STEP by STEP is the lesson.

Decision Tree for Luis

Step 1. So, let's look at a simple one. <u>Luis's goal is to do well in Math.</u> The problem is that he has Math class right before lunch, and he is often too hungry to pay attention. Math is hard and if he is hungry and distracted, it becomes impossible to listen and participate in class. He is totally frustrated. Luis has been told that he should have breakfast to avoid this problem. He never has breakfast and doesn't really believe that having breakfast will make a difference. However, Luis is willing to try it out and experiment with different breakfasts.

Step 2. So, the first question in the box on the left is Whether to have breakfast? The next column answers that question with NO and YES. Let's follow the NO branch. The next question is Hungry? The next column answers that question with NO and YES. Let's follow the NO branch first. Luis is not hungry. The question is Paying Attention? The next column answers that question with NO and YES.

Step 3. Then we go back to the second column that asked Hungry? The next column answers that question with NO and YES. Let's follow the YES branch this time. He is uncomfortable, paying attention? Again, we move next to the NO and YES boxes. NO says Not paying attention. YES, states that he is paying attention. Maybe Luis has particularly good self-control and can pay attention even if he is very hungry. The next step is to go back to Column 1, Having Breakfast? and then follow the YES answer. So, the next question is Healthy, nutritious breakfast? The next column answers that question with NO and YES. Let's follow the NO branch first. Let's again take the NO branch first since it is on top. Luis eats junk food. The question is Hungry? The next column answers that question with NO and YES. The last question is paying attention? The next column again answers that question with NO and YES.

Decision Tree for Luis

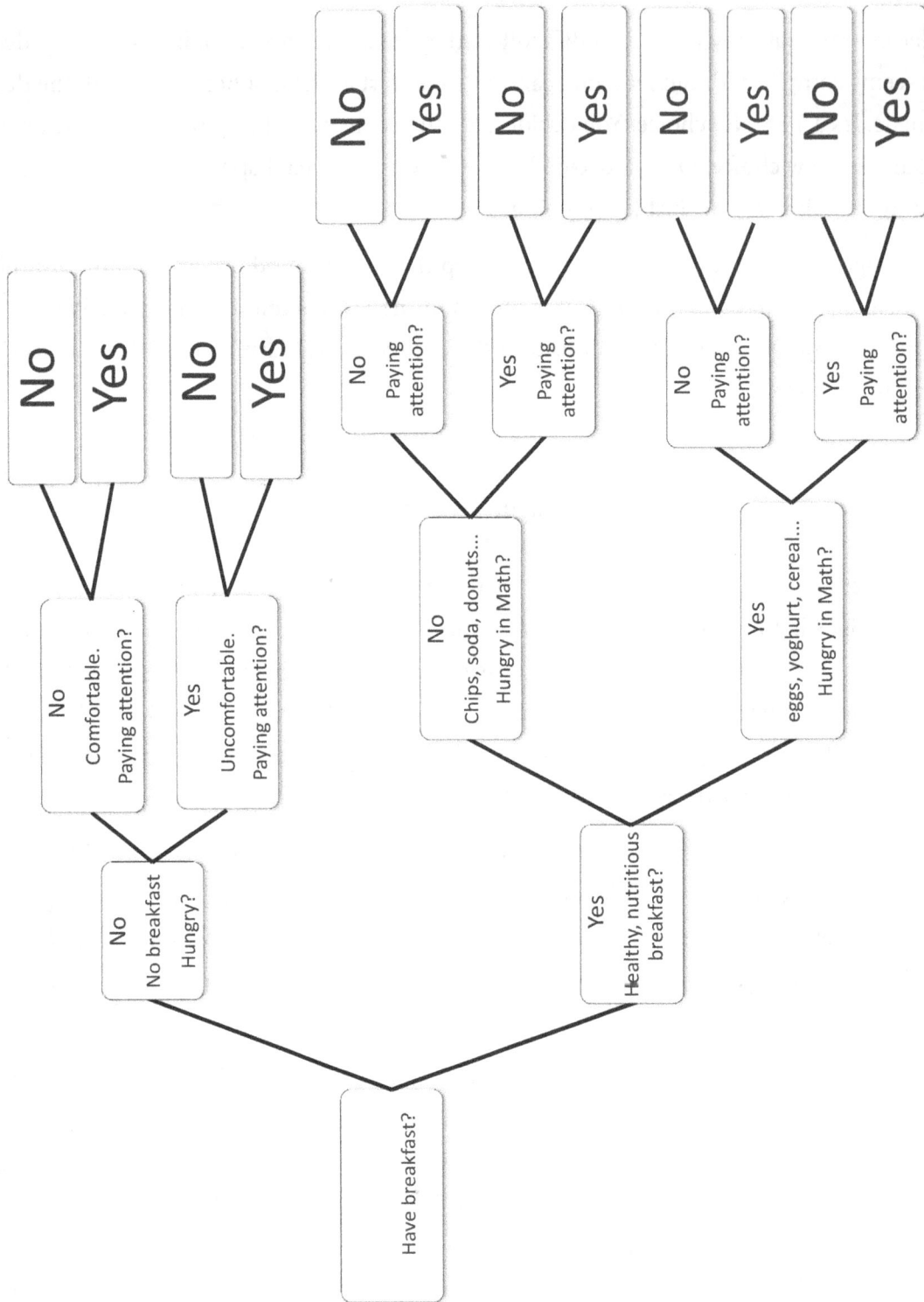

```
                                                    No
                                                    Yes
                                              Paying
                                              attention?
                                              No

                                                    No
                                                    Yes
                                              Paying
                                              attention?
                                              Yes
                                        Chips, soda, donuts…
                                        Hungry in Math?
                                        No

                                                    No
                                                    Yes
                                              Paying
                                              attention?
                                              No

                                                    No
                                                    Yes
                                              Paying
                                              attention?
                                              Yes
                                        eggs, yoghurt, cereal…
                                        Hungry in Math?
                                        Yes

        No
        Yes
  Comfortable.
  Paying attention?
  No

        No
        Yes
  Uncomfortable.
  Paying attention?
  Yes

            No breakfast
            Hungry?
            No

                            Healthy, nutritious
                            breakfast?
                            Yes

                    Have breakfast?
```

Decision Tree for Sha'anice

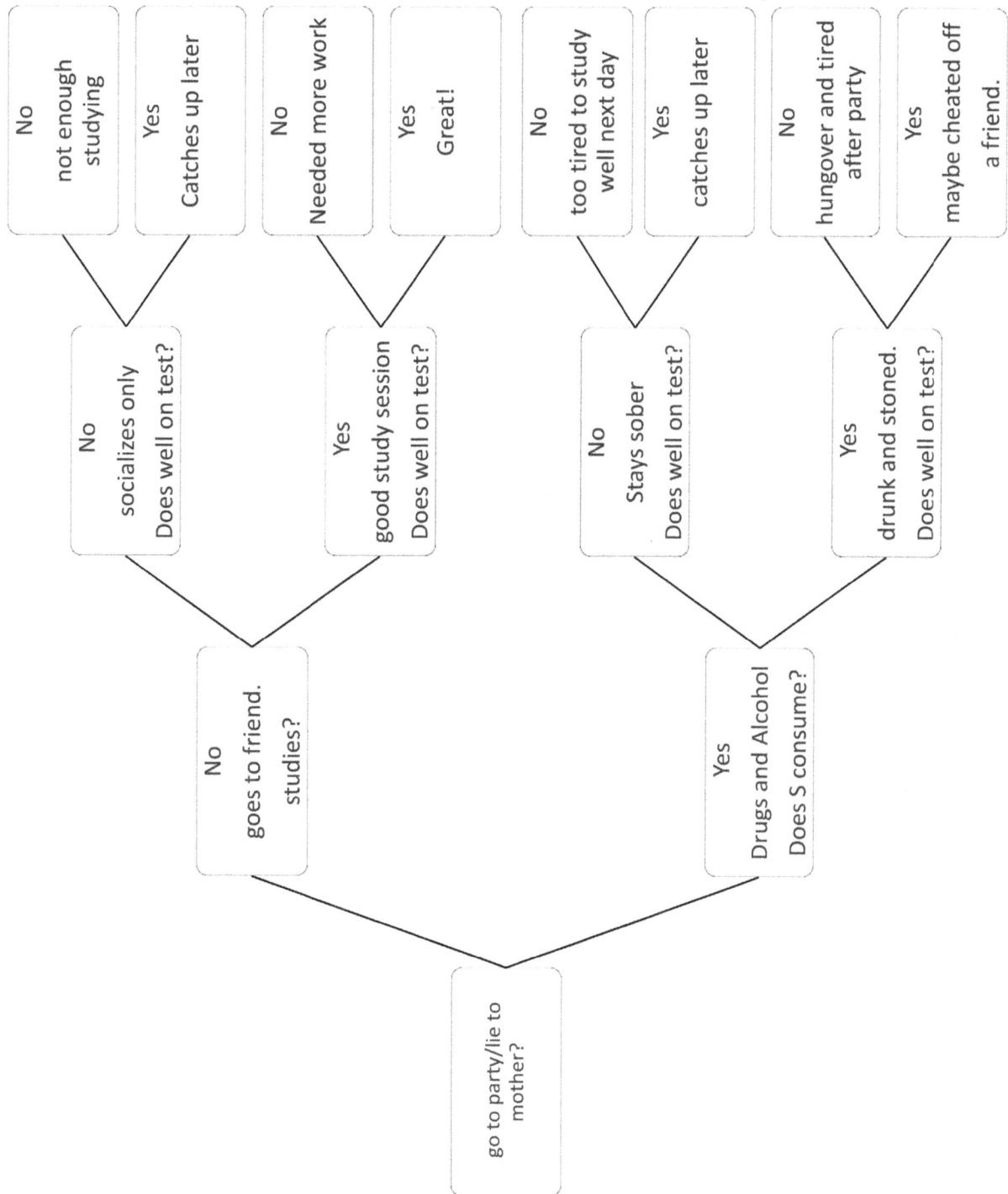

Decision Tree for Cameron

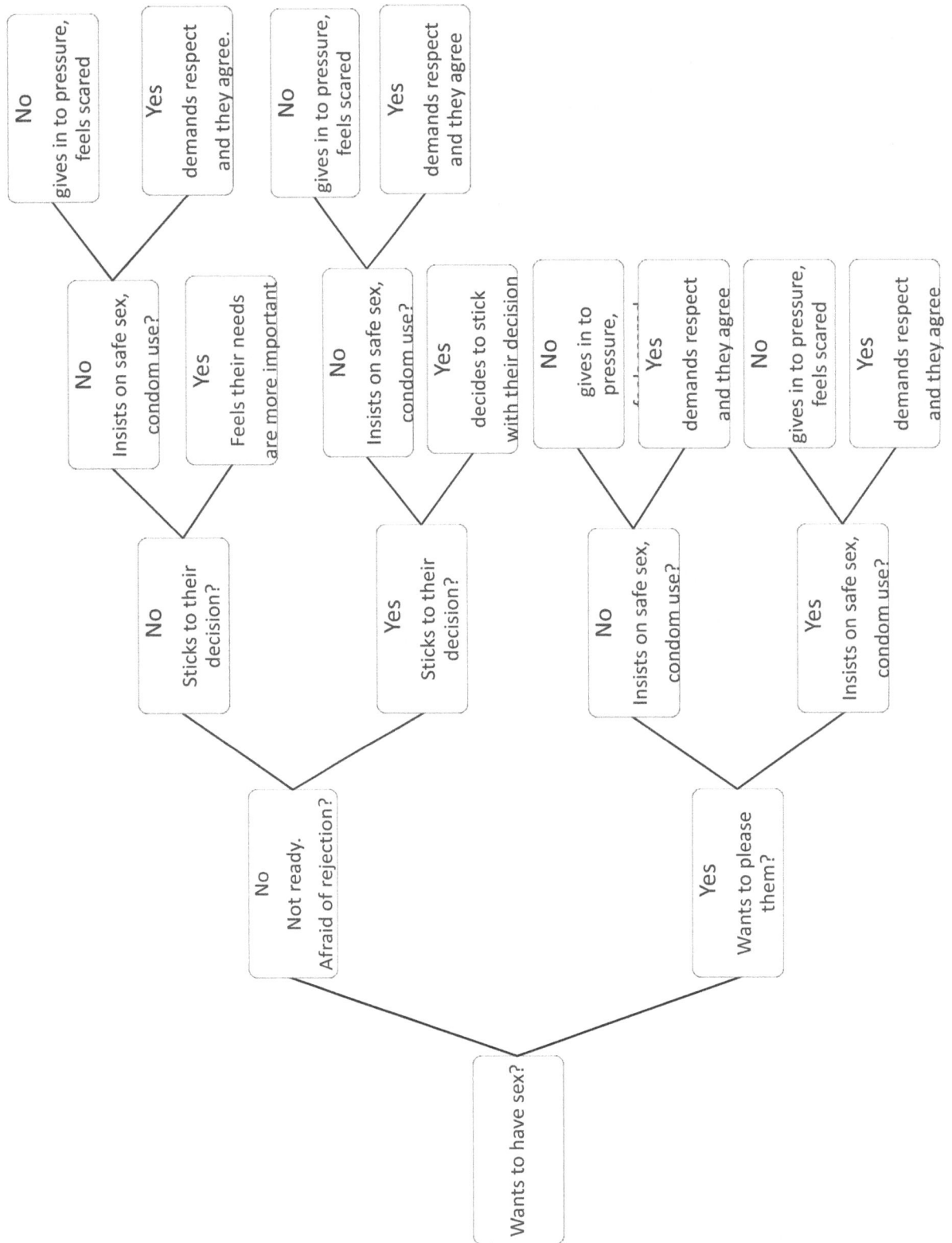

Blank Decision Tree

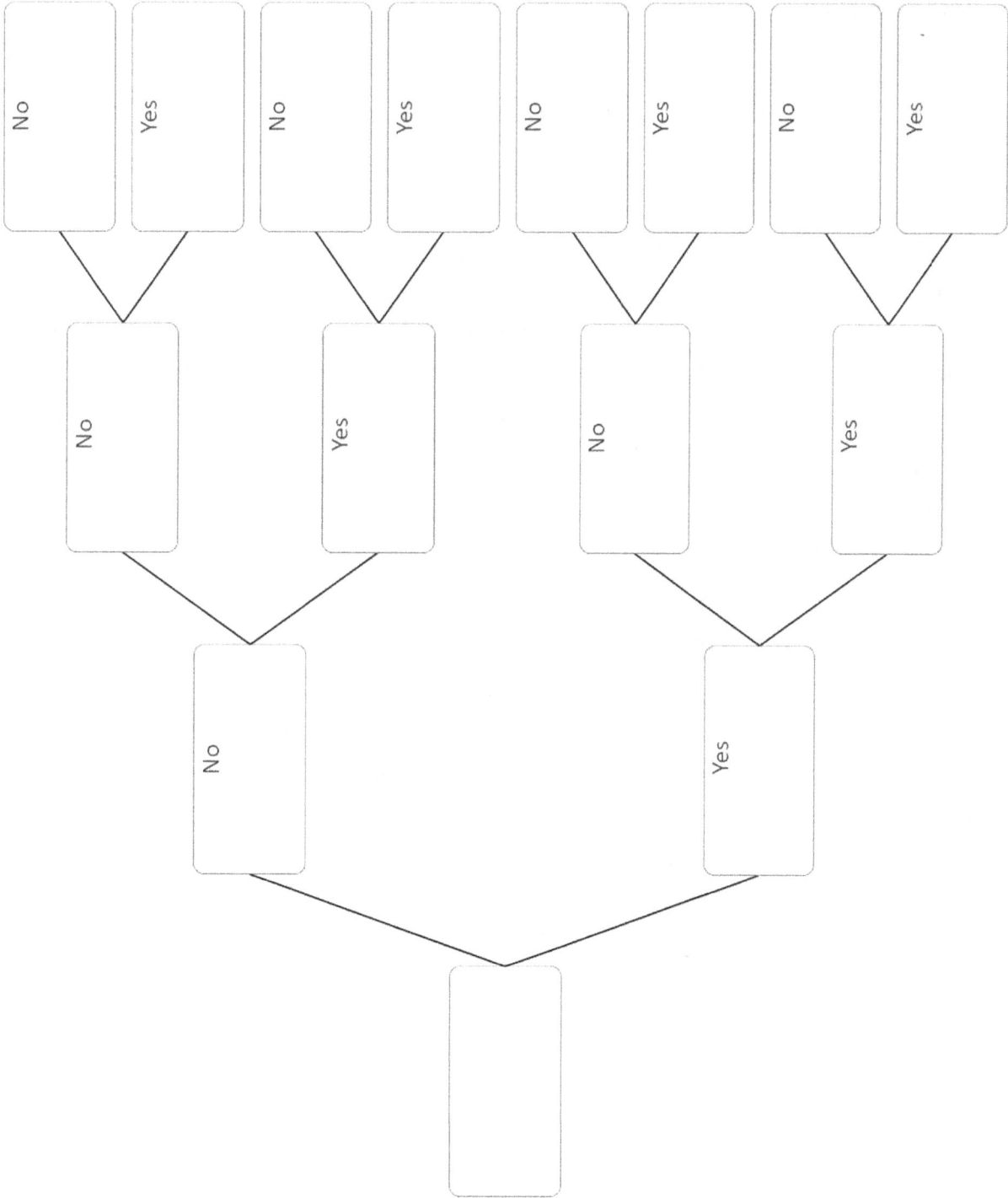

No | Yes | No | Yes | No | Yes | No | Yes

No | Yes | No | Yes

No | Yes

You can see that by looking at each step, you can make out what is likely to happen depending on your choices. Alternately, if Luis does experiment, he can record what did happen, whether he had breakfast or not.

Decision Tree for Sha'anice

Next, let's build a decision tree for <u>Sha'anice who had to decide between going to a forbidden party and studying.</u> If she decided to go to the party, she'd have to lie to her mother about studying with a friend. She knew that no one would be supervising the party. It was a secret. The party could be fun, but there might also be weed and beer present. Things could possibly get out of hand. A neighbor might call the police if the kids were rowdy. She might drink and smoke, risk her personal safety and engage in sex with a random partner.

Of course, you might say that she won't know this until after the party has happened, but the truth is that she (and you) can and need to think about it before hand. This way, she and you can make more knowing choices for yourselves.

Let's look at the decision tree I built for Sha'anice's decision about whether to go to the party/lie to her mother. Follow each branch from left to right, to its conclusion, just like you did with the Breakfast decision.

You can see that by looking at each step, you can make out what could happen depending on her choices. None of us knows the future but we can make good guesses and consider our path carefully. In the last box on the right, I suggest that the only way she could do well on the test if she skipped studying, went to the party, smoked and drank, is by cheating...she could not realistically do well (honestly) under those circumstances.

Remember that this is not about judging yourself but judging your decisions – it is about looking carefully at decisions and making the ones that work best for you.

Decision Tree for Cameron

We're going to look at one more. This one is going to be for <u>Cameron's difficult decision: whether to have sex with a romantic partner.</u> Cameron's partner may want to have sex, but Cameron is not sure. Does Cameron do it to please him or her? Is Cameron afraid of being rejected if he/she doesn't have sex with the partner? Does Cameron put his/her needs first? Does Cameron insist on safe sex? What are the consequences of each decision? See if you can follow that one without it being spelled out.

CHAPTER 2

Early Skills Lead to Self-Sufficiency

This chapter is about your childhood, the first twelve years of your life. They are the foundation that the rest of your life will be built on. Therefore, they are particularly important. While you probably were not self-aware during those years, many experiences were contributing to your development. Many readers will find it easy to ask parents about these early facts. However, teens and young adults living with guardians or other caregivers may find it challenging. I encourage you to try anyway, maybe after requesting permission to seek such information.

Part 1. Physical Development

We'll start with your physical development, starting with that most important period, in utero, in your mother's womb. You will quickly see that all these questions are important.

Your birth. Date_____; your weight _____your length _____

Were you a term baby (9 months pregnancy) _____; were there any problems with your

mother's pregnancy ? _____

If yes, what? _____

Were you premature? _____how many weeks? _____

Were you healthy? _____If not, what was wrong? _____

_____

_____

Were you hospitalized? _____for how long? _____

Part 2. The First Years of Your Life

There were many milestones. I hope you will be able to find out about them.

When did you first sit up? _____ Walk? _____

When did you learn to run? _____ skip? _____jump? _____

climb stairs? _____ go downstairs? _____

Say a few words? _____ Spoke in sentences? _____

At what age were you toilet trained: day _____ night _____?

Do your parents/caregivers tell you funny stories about you when you were little?

_____

_____

_____

Part 3. Elementary School Years

When did you first learn to read? _____ Do you read fluently? _____

When did you first learn how to write? _____

Can you write whole sentences? _____

Can you spell most words correctly? _____

When did you first learn how to count? _____add?_____ subtract?

_____ multiply? _____ divide?_____

Can you do fractions? _____decimals? _____percentages? _____

What was easy for you in school?

_____

What was hard for you in school?

_____

_____

Part 4. Social Development

This is more complicated. It will take a bit of self-awareness and honesty. Don't forget to be honest with yourself. This is private. No one needs to know but it is important to be straight with yourself so that you know yourself and what you want for yourself.

Exercise 1: Behavior with Parents/Caregivers

Did you learn to obey your parents/caregivers?_____

Did you throw temper tantrums when frustrated? _____

At what age did you stop? _____

Did you learn to talk to your parents/caregivers about what you needed _____

Were you allowed to speak up for yourself? _____

How did that feel? _____

Exercise 2: Behavior with Peers

Do you know how to take turns? _____

Do you know how to play fair with others? _____

Do you know how to win at a game and be nice about it? _____

Do you know how to lose at a game and be a good sport? _____

Can you give an example of when you lost at a game and were a good sport about it? _____

_____

_____

_____

Do you ever cheat at games? _____

How do you feel about that? _____

_____

Can you give an example of when you cheated at a game:

_____

How did the others react? _____

How did you feel about it? _____

Do you know how to stick to a project? _____

Do you know how to finish what you start? _____

Do a good job? _____

Can you give an example of when you completed a project that you started? _____

_____

_____

How did you feel about it? _____

Exercise 3: Behavior at School

Do you know how to pay attention in class? _____

Do you get in trouble for talking? _____

Do you get in trouble for being out of your seat? _____

Do you get in trouble for teasing a classmate? _____

Do you know to be honest? _____

Do you know to respect other kids' stuff? _____

Are there things you do that get you in trouble? _____

What are they? _____

Do you make them right? _____

How do you accept consequences? _____

Do you know when to ask for help from the teacher? _____

Do you ask for help when you don't understand? _____

Can you give an example of when you asked for help from a teacher? _____

_____

Did the teacher help? _____

Did you feel satisfied? _____

Do you know how to cooperate on a class or group project? _____

Do you make sure that you're doing a good share of the work? _____

Do you share ideas with others in the group? _____

How do you feel if they like your ideas? _____

If they don't? _____

Please give an example of what happened when you participated in a group activity that went well: What did you do? How did you feel about yourself? Others?

_____

_____

_____

Please give an example of what happened when you participated in a group activity that didn't go so well: what did you do? How did you feel about yourself? Others?

_____

_____

_____

Exercise 4: Behavior with Friends

Making good friends. Here, it is again important to be honest with yourself. Remember that this work is private: no one else needs to see it. You do not need to judge yourself, just acknowledge the truth.

Friends are special. They are people you can count on: Can your friends count on you? ____

_____

Friends are people who have your back. Do you have your friends' backs? _____

Friends are people that need your respect: do you respect your friends? _____

_____

Friends must not be pressured into doing your bidding: that is disrespectful. Do you pressure

your friends? _____

How does that work out? _____

Do not manipulate or trick your friends to get them to do what you want to them to do: it is disrespectful.

Do you do that? _____ How does it work out? _____

_____

How do you handle disagreements? Do you talk about things? Do you just get mad and

"drop" a friend? _____

_____

How do you make up after a fight with a friend? _____

_____

_____

Do you betray former friends by talking trash about them? _____

_____

_____

Do you spread rumors to get back at them? _____

_____

_____

Do you share things with others that you know you shouldn't? _____

_____

_____

* * *

Friends must treat YOU with respect, as well. This is especially important. It is essential to learn to pick people that become good friends.

Do you pick friends you can count on? _____

Do they have your back? _____

Do they treat you with respect? _____

Do they respect your things? _____

Your parents/caregivers?_____ Your pets? _____

Your other friends? _____

Do they pressure you to do things that you don't want to do? _____

_____

_____

Do they try to manipulate or trick you into doing what they want? _____

_____

_____

How do they handle disagreements? Do they talk about things? Do they just get mad and drop the friendship? How do they make up after a fight?

_____

_____

Do they betray you by gossiping about you? _____

_____

_____

Spreading rumors? _____

_____

Do they reveal things that they know they shouldn't? _____

_____

_____

Exercise 5: Looking at Your Friendships

Now you can look at some friendships that you have. Pick one friend at a time. Look at the above points and see how each friend fits. No one is perfect and neither are our friends. It is important to know your friends well and to understand how they relate to you and you relate to them.

Friend 1. What are their good points?

_____

_____

_____

_____

Friend 1. What are their weak points?

_____

_____

_____

_____

Friend 2. What are their good points?

_____

_____

_____

_____

Friend 2. What are their weak points?

_____

_____

_____

_____

Friend 3. What are their good points?

_____

_____

_____

_____

Friend 3. What are their weak points?

CHAPTER 3

_____

_____

_____

_____

New Skills Lead to Independence and Responsibility

Introduction

Congratulations on having entered the teen years. During the first twelve years of your life, your family and your teachers took care of teaching you everything you needed to know. I have included in this chapter the skills pre-teens need to learn to help them be ready for the teen years.

As you enter the teen years, it is now becoming your turn to take charge of yourself and your behavior. You're going to tackle the different areas of autonomy (which means self-governing or self-management). You will see that you make decisions about your behavior, decisions about personal choices, all the time.

You'll look at the different responsibilities that are now coming under your charge. You'll be amazed and maybe a little overwhelmed. However, none of this is learned overnight. You have time to get comfortable with them. You will feel yourself empowered as you learn to manage more and more of them.

Another important aspect of this work is that it is personal. I again recommend that you keep it private. Remember, this is your work and you are entitled to privacy. This will allow you to be honest with your current abilities and your need for mastery; no judgment is needed as you choose the person you want to become.

Workbook for Pre-Teens

Starting in the pre-teen years, these are the skills to be learned. These skills lead to growing independence:

Taking care of your personal hygiene

Getting your homework done by yourself

Doing your household chores without reminders

Other home responsibilities – taking care of pets, sports equipment, etc.

Managing responsibilities at school

Emotional coping and choices, autonomy

Self-management; self-soothing when distressed

Part 1. Personal Hygiene

This is important. It is essential to build good habits for taking care of yourself. You will feel good when you are taking care of yourself.

You may want to make yourself a check list of things that need to be done. This is often helpful until those things become a habit.

Washing your face every day

Taking a shower every one or two days

Shampooing your hair thoroughly

Brushing your teeth once or twice a day

Combing your hair at least once a day

Using deodorant if necessary

Washing your hands after using toilet

Washing your hands before eating or handling food

Washing your hands after eating or handling food

Changing underwear at least every other day

(wash it by hand in the sink if necessary: that's what we have always done)

You can use the weekly personal hygiene calendar provided in this chapter to list your responsibilities on the left and check off items as they get done. You will see that everyday has a morning and an evening space to check off.

In the guidebook, I talk about chaining activities so that you remember the sequence. It is easier to do things in an order that makes sense, than to remember each activity as a separate piece.

The following chains can be helpful. I offer an example first, sometimes with humor. Then I ask for you to list the links of your chain. It is ok if they are the same as mine if they work for your needs.

Morning Routine Example	**My Morning Routine**
Link 1: I wake up when my alarm goes off	Link 1: _____
Link 2: I get up without hitting snooze too much	Link 2: _____
Link 3: I get dressed	Link 3: _____
Link 4: I eat breakfast, maybe pop-tarts or eggs	Link 4: _____
Link 5: I brush my teeth	Link 5: _____
Link 6: I wash my face	Link 6: _____
Link 7: I unplug my school computer and put it in my backpack	Link 7: _____
Link 8: I make sure my homework is all in my backpack	Link 8: _____
Link 9: I get a snack from the kitchen and put it in my backpack	Link 9: _____
Link 10: I make sure I have my lunch or lunch money	Link 10: _____
Link 11: I make my bed	Link 11: _____
Link 12: I make sure the lights are out in my room	Link 12: _____
Link 13: I say goodbye	Link 13: _____
Link 14: I walk out to the bus stop	Link 14: _____
Link 15: I get on the bus, prepared to have a great day at school!	Link 15: _____

Night Routine Example

Link 1: I start getting ready an hour before bedtime

Link 2: I pick out my PJs

Link 3: I get a towel

Link 4: I remove my makeup

Link 5: I get undressed in the bathroom

Link 6: I put my dirty clothes in the hamper

Link 7: I take a shower

Link 8: I dry off and get dressed in my PJs

Link 9: I brush my teeth

Link 10: I pick out a good book or notepad

Link 11: I say goodnight to my family

Link 12: I read or draw in my notepad

Link 13: I text my friends goodnight

Link 14: I turn out the lights

Link 15: I get a good night's sleep so I can have a great day tomorrow!

My Night Routine

Link 1: _____

_____

Link 2: _____

_____

Link 3: _____

_____

Link 4: _____

_____

Link 5: _____

_____

Link 6: _____

_____

Link 7: _____

_____

Link 8: _____

_____

Link 9: _____

_____

Link 10: _____

_____

Link 11: _____

_____

Link 12: _____

_____

Link 13: _____

_____

Link 14: _____

_____

Link 15: _____

_____

WEEKLY PERSONAL HYGIENE CALENDAR														
		MONDAY		TUESDAY		WEDNESDAY		THURSDAY		FRIDAY		SATURDAY		SUNDAY
		AM	PM	AM	PM	AM	PM	AM	PM	AM	PM	AM	PM	AM	PM
Self-Care														

Part 2. Managing Homework

This is about managing yourself in the world. You have responsibilities. At school, you're expected to get your work done. The teacher teaches the lesson. You are expected to pay attention and to learn what is being taught.

This is an active process. Just listening won't do it. You must take it in and think about what is being taught. You need to understand. (If you don't understand, you need to speak up – we'll get to that later). You do this work mostly by yourself.

You're also given work to do at home or after school to make sure that you are understanding the material being taught and remembering it. Homework is showing you have learned the lesson and can apply it. Sometimes, you need help with some of it. Maybe your parents/caregivers or siblings can help. Maybe a teacher can help after school or during study hall.

Here is a checklist (or chain) for getting your homework done and turned in on time:

Write down the assignments

Bring the right books home or to after-school tutorials

Start on your homework early to have time to finish it

Take little breaks to help you refresh

Do homework without being prodded into it

Do it without supervision

Request help when needed

Review lesson with caregiver if needed

Make sure you understand the material

Make sure you understand what's being asked of you

Resume working on your own as soon as possible

Do not let others do your work, steal your success

Complete your work

Enjoy feeling good about yourself

Pack up your work to keep it safe

Place it in your backpack, ready to be handed in

Start projects early; give yourself plenty of time

Check that you have the needed materials

Do the best job you can: you deserve success

Enjoy the feeling of accomplishment

Enjoy receiving a good grade for the work

The good feeling that comes from taking care of yourself by getting your work done on time and as well as you can is something everyone needs to enjoy. It is a special feeling. We call it empowerment: when we feel in charge of ourselves and our lives.

You can use the Identity Scale to show your progress. You can see where you are moving towards your goals for yourself.

Homework Chain Example	**Your Homework Chain**
Link 1: I come home from school	Link 1. _____
Link 2: I put my backpack on hook by the door	Link 2:_____
	_____
Link 3: I have a snack	Link 3:_____
Link 4: I take a short break to watch YouTube	Link 4:_____
	_____
Link 5: I take my backpack to the kitchen table	Link 5:_____
	_____
Link 6: I take out planner to see homework due	Link 6:_____
	_____
Link 7: I choose the assignment to work on first	Link 7:_____
	_____
Link 8: I take out what I need to get it done (Binder, textbook, worksheets)	Link 8:_____
	_____
Link 9: I get it done, and ask for help if needed	Link 9:_____
	_____
Link 10: I put the papers away, safe from pets	Link 10:_____
	_____
Link 11: Same thing with the next assignment	Link 11:_____
	_____
Link 12: When I'm done, I put it all away in my backpack	Link 12:_____
	_____
Link 13: I plug in my school computer so it will be charged for the next day	Link 13:_____
	_____
Link 14: I put the backpack back on the hook, ready for tomorrow	Link 14:_____
	_____
Link 15: In the morning, I make sure to put my computer back in the backpack	Link 15:_____
	_____

Part 3. Household Chores and Responsibilities

Taking care of your things and your space:

Your clothes. Maybe help with folding your clothes, putting away your laundry.

Pick up your clothes, hang them up or put them in the wash. Learn to do laundry.

Prepare your clothes for outings, school days. For school days, prepare them the night before.

Keep your room in order. Pick up your toys and stuff. Make your bed. Keep your desk and things in order.

Dust your furniture. Vacuum your room. Sweep your floor.

Helping with household chores. This is the time to take on regular chore assignments that are expected of you and become your responsibility. This is to help you become accountable and responsible.

Wash dishes as needed.

Set and clear the table.

Help with dusting, vacuuming, sweeping floor.

Help with pets. Feed and clean after them.

Walk dogs at least once a day.

Help with food shopping, putting things away.

Help with meal preparation, planning, cooking, serving.

Help with gardening chores.

Here again, it feels good to feel on top of things. In control. Pleased with the space you create for yourself.

WEEKLY CHORES CALENDAR

Chore	MONDAY		TUESDAY		WEDNESDAY		THURSDAY		FRIDAY		SATURDAY		SUNDAY	
	AM	PM	AM	PM	AM	PM	AM	PM	AM	PM	AM	PM	AM	PM

Daily Chores Example   **My Daily Chores**

Link 1: I pick up my room   Link 1: _____

                                            _____

Link 2: I make the bed   Link 2: _____

                                            _____

Link 3: I turn out the bedroom light   Link 3: _____

                                            _____

Link 4: I feed the dog   Link 4: _____

                                            _____

Link 5: I clean bathroom   Link 5: _____

                                            _____

Link 6: After school, I walk the dogs   Link 6: _____

                                            _____

Link 7: I fold the laundry   Link 7: _____

                                            _____

Link 8: I help make dinner   Link 8: _____

                                            _____

Link 9: I set the table   Link 9: _____

                                            _____

Link 10: I clear the table   Link 10: _____

                                            _____

Link 11: I do dishes, clean the kitchen counter   Link 11: _____

                                            _____

Link 12: I feed the dogs   Link 12: _____

                                            _____

Link 13: I start my laundry when needed   Link 13: _____

                                            _____

Link 14: I pick up my things around the house   Link 14: _____

                                            _____

Link 15: I make sure my room is ready for the next day   Link 15: _____

                                            _____

Weekend Chores Example	**My Weekend Chores**
Link 1: I pick up my room	Link 1: _____
	_____
Link 2: I make the bed	Link 2: _____
	_____
Link 3: I dust my bedroom furniture	Link 3: _____
	_____
Link 4: I sweep or vacuum my room	Link 4: _____
	_____
Link 5: I vacuum the living room	Link 5: _____
	_____
Link 6: I dust the living room furniture	Link 6: _____
	_____
Link 7: I sweep the kitchen	Link 7: _____
	_____
Link 8: I take the dogs for a run	Link 8: _____
	_____
Link 9: I clean my bathroom	Link 9: _____
	_____
Link 10: I pick up the backyard	Link 10: _____
	_____
Link 11: I milk the cows!	Link 11: _____
	_____
Link 12: I churn the butter for the week!	Link 12: _____
	_____
Link 13: I bale the hay!	Link 13: _____
	_____
Link 14: I round up the cattle!	Link 14: _____
	_____
Link 15: I feed the pigs!	Link 15: _____
	_____
☺ Those were the good, old days!	

Part 4. Managing Yourself with Brothers and Sisters

As you get past ten years of age, you may be asked to stay alone at home or even to baby sit a younger brother or sister. Both are big responsibilities. You are now expected to keep yourself safe and your siblings as well.

Knowing to stay inside the house

Keeping apartment or house doors locked

Not allowing anyone to enter or leave the home

Avoiding dangerous behaviors such as playing with matches or other fire

Keeping away from knives and other possible weapons

No hitting or threatening your brothers and sisters

Keeping them occupied with play or schoolwork

Needing to feed yourself and them

Having enough water to drink

Obeying all house rules, including not touching liquor or cigarettes

Part 5. Managing Responsibilities at School: Taking Charge of Your Own Learning

This is often a big challenge for pre-teens. However, this is the time to make sure you are reading well and understanding and managing math. These two subjects are the ones that will take you to your goals or get in the way of your dreams if they are not mastered.

1. Reading is a basic skill that must be practiced every day. If you're having problems, there are teachers to help at school, your parents or caregivers and siblings to help at home. Sometimes, after school programs also provide help.

2. The way you practice reading is:

You read carefully.

You look up words you don't know.

You stop when you don't understand and re-read till you understand.

Finally, you stop and tell yourself what you have just read.

If you can't remember, you must re-read, paying more attention.

If you didn't get it, you must re-read and make sure you understand.

This sounds like a big burden but if you don't take in what you read, you have wasted your time and effort. It's worse than if you hadn't read it because you are frustrated.

3. Math is just as important. You must get it, or it will stop you in your tracks.

    Learn the basics: to add and subtract, divide and multiply.

    Learn your tables so that you are fluent when you work.

    Learn fractions and percentiles.

If you have a computer at home, get on it and learn it there, doing whatever exercises you can find.

If you don't have a computer at home, you can do it after school in the library. You can also do it on paper. There were no computers when millions of us learned our tables and we learned them anyway. Mostly by repetition – that's really the best way. It becomes like a song in your head: the answers just pop out, without your even thinking about them.

4. If you have difficulties with learning, sometimes due to ADHD or Dyslexia, there is always help in the schools. There are special classes, special tutors, and other resources needed.

5. Sometimes, your life is difficult, and you may suffer from emotional difficulties; for these situations, there is help with counselors, psychologists, at school and in the community.

Even if you have difficulties, it is important to learn these two basic skills as best as you can – reading and math – the world will open before you, no matter what other problems there are. If you don't, many doors will be closed and stay closed until you learn those skills. Lots of colleges have special programs to help students catch up and enjoy success in their life. REMEMBER, IT'S NEVER TOO LATE!

6. Other skills to learn at school:

    *   In the classroom:

        Obeying classroom and group rules

        Cooperating with other students when needed

        Respecting others' space and their work

        Staying on task and doing your work as best as you can

    *   On the playground, or in the school yard:

        Taking turns, cooperating in games with others

Not allowing others to bully you or bullying others to get your way

Leadership skills include flexibility and kindness to others

Be a follower sometimes and go along when wise

Avoid challenges to do dangerous or stupid things

Avoid doing dumb things just to be noticed by others

It is so important to take charge of your life at school. Stop hating school and understand that this is your future. When you succeed here, you also succeed in your life. Thus, this is crucial to your success. You can succeed! (In a later chapter, you'll learn how to get the help you need).

Part 6. Emotional Coping and Choices; Autonomy

It is important to take care of yourself, your feelings, your emotions. You must acknowledge your feelings, identify them. Feelings are natural and essential: they tell you how you are reacting to a situation. You must always respect your "gut" feelings; they allow you to trust someone or they warn you that something doesn't feel right.

Exercise 1: Where do you feel your emotions? Some are felt in the head, the heart, the stomach, the gut, the clenched fists.

a. Joy or happiness _____

b. Pleasure or satisfaction _____

c. Trust _____

d. Anger _____

e. Fear _____

f. Irritation _____

g. Frustration _____

h. Panic _____

Exercise 2: Once feelings are acknowledged and understood, then you can look at your behavior. Are you aware of choosing your behavior? Most pre-teens are not. They only react to what is happening to them. So, here is an exercise to help you become more aware of how you act.

How do you act? What do you do?

a. When happy, I _____

b. When pleased, satisfied, I _____

c. When trusting, I _____

d. When angry, I _____

e. When afraid, I _____

f. When irritated, I _____

g. When frustrated, I _____

h. When panicking, I _____

Exercise 3: How do you feel about your behavior when you react to others? How do you feel about the results? How do you feel about the consequences?

Example: One of the school bullies is coming towards you. What are you expecting? How might you react? How do you then feel about it? Let's explore the possibilities.

I would feel frustrated if: _____

_____

_____

I would feel angry if: _____

_____

_____

I would feel afraid if: _____

_____

_____

I would feel embarrassed if: _____

_____

_____

Maybe you can learn to take your time, to decide on your action. Some ways to give yourself time to think and choose your actions are:

I will count to ten

I take a silent moment to hear my inner voice

I don't want to let him or her push my buttons

I don't want to get in trouble

He's stronger than me

I won't let her bully me

I need to walk away

I need to remember what's important

Take a moment to choose your behavior

I am taking charge of this situation

I can look her in the eye, shrug my shoulders, and walk away

I can tell he's itching for a fight, but I don't have to fight

I can tell her that I understand

I can give him a hug

I can say that I will think about what she said

Exercise 4: Learning to ACT instead of RE-ACTING

Can you think of a time when you just reacted to an event? How did it work out? Were you okay with how things turned out? If not, what do you wish you had done? How could you have chosen that behavior?

_____

_____

_____

_____

Can you think of a time when you took the time to choose your behavior in responding to someone? What was going on? What did you choose to do? How did it turn out? Did you feel good about it, about yourself?

_____

_____

_____

_____

Which of the behaviors mentioned above are you likely to try? Why do you think it will work for you?

_____

_____

_____

_____

Part 7. Self-Management; Self-Soothing

It is also important to take care of yourself when things don't go your way. Self-management means taking care of your behavior; self-soothing means taking care of yourself when you're hurting.

In the previous sections, you learned about self-management: personal hygiene, responsibilities at home and at school, helping yourself catch up or keep up in school, taking care of brothers and sisters. Here, you'll be learning to take care of yourself when you're hurting.

Everyone suffers disappointments, frustrations, losses; it is essential to take care of yourself. When you were little, you had a stuffed toy or a blanket you went to when you needed comforting. Some people have a physical place they go to or sometimes a place in their mind. Sometimes, there is someone they can always go to for comfort. Sometimes, they play or listen to music, talk to a friend, text with a friend, check on social media, watch a favorite program, do a jigsaw puzzle, in order to find comfort and regain their balance, their center. Sometimes, people engage in behaviors that help them manage the pain right then but are only arousing more pain down the road: cutting, drinking alcohol, doing drugs, running away, engaging in risky behaviors.

Exercise 1: What are things that you do when you are seeking comfort?

a. _____

b. _____

c. _____

d. _____

Exercise 2: Are there negative or risky behaviors that you sometimes engage in?

a. _____

b. _____

c. _____

Exercise 3: Can you think of things that you'd like to do but haven't tried?

a. _____

b. _____

c. _____

It is important to take care of yourself; guide your life the way you want it to be. Attend to your needs. Listen to that inner voice that tells you what's right for you. So, be friendly and fair but don't do things just to please others, just so they'll "like" you. They won't. They'll just take advantage of you, use you. People like and respect people who stand up for themselves, who stay true to themselves, who let them know how they truly feel.

Don't be a bully either. No one will like you even if you feel a bit powerful. Others will seem to join you, but they do it because they're afraid of you. But bullies aren't strong: they're afraid that people won't like them anyway and they're angry. So, they're out to show others. Unfortunately, it doesn't help them feel better about themselves. Just the opposite. This proves to them that they can't make friends.

The only way to make friends is to be happy with who you are and letting others get to know you. Happy people always have friends: they're like magnets. So, what if you aren't happy. You're having a hard time at home. You're having a hard time at school. So, how can you be happy?

The truth is that being happy with yourself is separate from being happy about your circumstances. Being happy with yourself is an attitude, a being in touch with your inner self, and taking good care of yourself. This book aims to teach you how to be happy with yourself.

Finally, if we wait for things to be different, it never happens. If you're having a hard time at school, you can work on your skills and get better. You can get help to do that. It takes courage to ask questions in class or to go to an afterschool tutorial. But as you get better at school, you will find yourself happier and more friendly.

When things are hard at home, you can also get help. You can talk to teachers and counselors at school. If things are seriously bad at home, sometimes you end up living somewhere else, somewhere where you're safe and taken care of. It's not an easy route, but it can really help a young person to a much better life.

Workbook for the Early Teen Years

Part 1. Know What You Want for Your Life

Get acquainted with your identity. Become aware of how you appear to the world. Look at your Identity Scale and then your Behavior Scale. How do you think about yourself? What do you see when you look in the mirror? When you are young, it is as unclear for you as it is for those teens on the book's cover. It becomes clearer and clearer as you learn to be aware of yourself, of who you are, of what you do.

Let's look at what is important to you. This is especially important as it guides your choices.

Ranking needs and desires, starting with 1 for "most important," down to 5 for "much less important." It's ok to have several things at each level of importance. Rank only the ones that matter to you.

_____social success, being popular

_____school success, good grades

_____being good at sports

_____helping your family

_____holding a job and having money

_____being a leader in your community

_____involvement with church or community organization

_____getting into college

_____being in a gang, feeling you belong in a group

_____being a leader in your classroom

_____nothing matters to me

_____experimenting with drugs

_____quitting school

_____running away from home

_____having a boyfriend or girlfriend

_____being sexually active

_____having a baby/child of your own

Not all of these goals will take you towards your dream. Some will lead you away from your goals and dreams. When your desire takes you away from your goals, it is most important to remember your dreams. This may help you go in a more positive direction.

If you feel that you can't make that happen for you, then it is likely time to get help from counselors at school or in the community. You are entitled to dreams and success in following them.

Part 2. Are there Obstacles in Your Life?

Do you have good momentum, or do you shrink back from moving forward in fear or anger? For many teens and young adults, moving forward is a challenge. They are often held back by inner obstacles, such as fear and anger. They are sometimes burdened with "outer" obstacles that make their life more challenging, obstacles in their performance. These might be learning disabilities, or even physical challenges. There are also obstacles in their environment (these will be handled in more detail in a later chapter).

When Fear Gets in the Way

What might make you move away from your dreams for yourself? Even those teens that believe they have no dreams do have dreams which are often buried deep inside of them. Some obstacles are inside us and we'll start by looking at what you need to do to overcome inner blocks to your success.

A lot of the time, it is your fear and your anger that rob you of having dreams and pursuing them. It is most important for you to know your fears and anger.

When fear is guiding you. It is important to face your fears and find ways to move forward. Let's look at the common fears that get in the way.

We need to become more courageous. COURAGEOUS means that we challenge and overcome our fears, not that they disappear.

Starting with little steps. To build up your courage, you need to:

Acknowledge your fear, face your fear, and work to get past it. Being courageous doesn't mean having no fear, it means doing things despite the fear.

Always start with the easiest thing to build up your confidence. Remember there is no magic, but you can do the work of becoming who you want to be.

Exercise 1: My first fear to overcome is:

_____

_____

What can I do to challenge it and conquer it?

_____

_____

Did I try that?

_____

_____

Did I succeed in doing it? (If not, don't give up. Try another approach).

_____

_____

How did I feel after that?

_____

_____

You can go back to the Identity Scale and see if you want to move the button for that quality.

Exercise 2: My next fear to overcome is:

_____

_____

What can I do to challenge it and conquer it?

_____

_____

Did I try that?

_____

_____

Did I succeed in doing it? (If not, don't give up. You can always try other ways)

_____

_____

How did I feel after that?

_____

_____

You can go back to the Identity Scale and see if you want to move the button for that quality.

When Anger Gets in the Way

Sometimes, it's anger that gets in the way of accomplishing our goals. Anger is especially important. It is our reaction to fear and pain. Looking at our anger often takes us back to our fear and to what hurts us.

Anger is often accompanied by despair and giving up. So, it is essential to know and understand your anger and then figure out how to use that energy to get you past the anger. (More in Chapter 9).

Begin by figuring out the source of your anger. What are you angry about? Are you angry with your school experience? Are you angry with parents or caregivers? Your home situation? Are you angry with the way society treats you? Angry with the way the world treats you? Are you angry with God?

Exercise 3: Let's take them one at a time. Maybe you can figure out how to manage.

1. Angry at school? Angry with schoolmates? Why?

   a. You're being bullied. What can you do?

      Would you report it to teachers?

      _____

      Could you ignore the bully? Walk away?

      _____

Do you want to fight the bullies?

_____

Can you take care of yourself (self-soothing) and go on with your day?

_____

Can you keep your goal in mind, keep moving forward?

_____

b. You feel that you can't succeed at school

Do you compare yourself to others? Does it help?

_____

Could you work harder? Get the help you need?

_____

Do you want to do better? Would you make it happen?

_____

Can you keep your goal in mind, keep moving forward?

_____

c. Others are more popular than you are.

Are you usually friendly with others?

_____

Are you a good friend?

_____

Are you a leader or a follower? Or maybe a loner?

_____

Can you look at your qualities on the Identity Scale?

_____

Can you see what you need to improve?

_____

2. Angry with parents/caregivers? Start by identifying why you are angry.

Do they treat you well?

_____

_____

Are they fair?

_____

_____

Are they kind?

_____

_____

Are they helpful?

_____

_____

Do they take care of you?

_____

_____

Do they provide a good home?

_____

_____

Do you feel safe at home?

_____

_____

Is there enough food for everyone?

_____

_____

Do you have a place to sleep? Do your homework?

_____

_____

What are your responsibilities at home?

_____

_____

_____

Too many chores, assignments?

_____

_____

_____

Not enough chores, responsibilities?

_____

_____

Are there large problems at home?

_____

_____

_____

When there are large problems at home, problems you're having a hard time coping with, it is important to get help.

Start by identifying people you can get help from:

A trusted relative

A trusted neighbor

A Counselor at school

A Psychologist at school

A church leader or trusted person

Helpers in community shelters

Have the courage to get help from CPS

3. Angry with society and the world. This is a real and difficult issue, one that often needs adults to intervene. Unfortunately, it takes a long time for change to come about.

   Lots of people think that society is not fair, and it often is not.

   Seeking justice, avoiding prejudice and racism is exceedingly difficult.

   People are marching in the streets to demand more justice

   There are groups that can help.

   You can steel yourself against injustice and keep moving ahead – every little step helps you reach your goal.

   You can be determined to take your place in the world, helping others do it, too.

4. Angry with God

   People think it's not fair that they have such challenges.

   Other people think God is testing them...that He wants them to be stronger. That's a better attitude. Respond to the challenges

   So many people have succeeded despite great challenges, or maybe because of them. They went full steam ahead, convinced of their power to overcome. We call them heroes, but everyone can be a hero.

   They succeed because they do the work of finding their way forward.

Become your own hero and you'll soon find yourself a popular leader!

When Disabilities Get in the Way

Sometimes, in addition to fear and anger, some teens and young adults feel limited because they have a disability. They sometimes feel that it's not fair, that they should not have it so hard. But, here again, it is up to you to manage your situation. Of course, there are sources of help, but it is up to you to find the strength to manage with your disability and live a good life.

Do you have a disability? Again, it's nobody's fault. Everyone has different challenges.

Exercise 4: Here you can look at your own situation.

   Many teens and young adults struggle with challenges. What are yours?

   _____

   _____

Are you getting the support you need at home?

_____

_____

Are you getting help at school and in the community?

_____

_____

Are you able to provide your own encouragement and support when it's difficult?

_____

_____

Getting needed support for your situation at school

    Schools do their best to provide educational support

    For reading and learning disabilities

    For ADHD and attention issues

    For social behavior disabilities

    For physical disabilities

    Public and private medicine offer services to all

Yes, this is an area where there are wide differences in services for the rich and the poor. Sometimes, you and your parents or caretakers need to fight for proper service. It's important to learn what you need, what resources there are, and to demand what is due you. Remember, success depends on your taking care of yourself. You're entitled to help and good treatment.

Part 3. Thinking about Your Future as an Adult

    Do you have a dream about what you want to do?

    Do you have a solid idea of the person you want to become?

    Do you have a plan for how to get there?

    Or do you have no idea what you might want to do?

    Are you afraid that you won't be good at anything?

    Have you been told you won't amount to much?

Do you avoid thinking about the future because it's just too complicated?

Or do you already know that you will go into a trade with a relative, or work in your parent's or caregiver's business?

Maybe you want to go into the Armed Forces like your cousin did.

Whatever your answer is, the truth is that you have a future to think about. It is your future. It is important to give it much thought so that you can succeed at making your dreams come true.

* * *

Today's reality is that there are many more possibilities than a century ago, but it is also much more complicated. A century ago, most people could get the skills they needed when they finished the sixth grade.

Today, you need to get through the twelfth grade to get basic needed skills. And that is for the most common and least paying jobs. If you want to go further in life, you must go to a technical school or junior college.

Many people go to college to get a degree to get a job that will give them a good living. Some people go beyond college to become professionals. All these choices are open to you and everyone. Some have an easier time to follow a long path, some a harder time. Still, it is available to all.

Don't forget: those professions need people to fill those positions.

Why not you? Anyone can become a doctor or a lawyer, or a scientist, or a psychologist, or a nurse, or even college professors.

Yes, it takes some smarts, but it mostly takes work and determination. This is where you come in: you need to decide what you want to reach for. Nothing is impossible. Any job can be yours if you work for it long and hard enough.

So, now is your chance to start dreaming and preparing yourself for an exciting future.

We also need to think that we live longer than we used to. We may be happy with a trade or an unskilled job now but then decide down the line that it's not enough.

Fortunately, we can always decide to move forward, maybe get a GED and get into a junior college, which can then lead to a four-year college and then professional schools...the roads are never closed. It is up to each one of us to keep looking ahead and choose our goals.

So, with that long road ahead, it is essential to develop good basic skills in math and language. I cannot repeat that enough. I will assume that you already manage to keep up with homework and class assignments.

If not, I encourage you to look at the Workbook for Pre-teens section where I encourage building those good habits. However, even if you have been keeping up, it is becoming harder and harder.

Exercise: What do you do to help yourself succeed?

Do you participate in class?

_____

_____

Do you ask questions?

_____

_____

Do you seek help before and after school?

_____

_____

Do you ask help from friends and relatives?

_____

_____

Do you use Khan Academy or YouTube videos to help you understand and learn?

_____

_____

Does your school district offer online help? Many of them do.

_____

_____

Do you go online and work up exercises for math?

_____

_____

Do you go online and work up reading and language exercises?

_____

_____

Do you do the same for other subjects?

_____

_____

* * *

As you work at the subjects being taught in school, you might come to think that you really enjoy math, or science, or history, or art, or sports.

That's the beginning of thinking about what you might want to do with your life. There is something you like; maybe you will keep liking it enough to want to engage in that activity or field as you leave high school.

Maybe you can win a scholarship with sports and then study a subject that really interests you. Or you may want to stay with the sport and become a professional player and then a coach...All the roads are open if you can get yourself motivated to go for the gold!

Let me repeat here that there are so many good sites on the Internet to get the coaching, review, help with all school subjects, that you need. Many school districts have their course work and exercises online for to you to log into. One helpful resource is Khan Academy which teaches everything in detail. You must pay attention and be patient, but you WILL understand what is being taught. YouTube has tons of material to teach anything you want to learn, at the high school and college level. Many colleges offer free courses.

You will see that you too can learn...then you can feel great satisfaction and even confidence that you can succeed.

* * *

Sadly, young people feel that school subjects are useless, that they won't need to know that stuff later. So, why should you know that stuff? Well, first, you need to understand what others on tv and online are talking about. Second, you need to be able to decide what makes sense and what doesn't. Many TV ads and magazine ads take advantage of people's not reasoning through their message. They assume that they can fool the listener or the reader into buying their product. Watch out! It's always Buyer Beware. It is up to you to sort through all these ads and decide for yourself what is useful and what is not.

* * *

The same is true for political issues. There is so much talk out there. As I write this, there is a busy presidential campaign going on. It is essential to understand what people are saying, what is true, what is not, what makes sense…

Do you know that the goal of the campaigns is often to get people fired up about issues and not really thinking things through? We all feel passionate about the issues, but do we know what promises are reasonable and realistic and which are not? No one is going to tell us. We listen to all kinds of opinions on both sides and it's hard to tell where to stand.

How does this relate to math and language? Well, those teach us how to think things through for ourselves. Science gives us an understanding of the material world. History can give us perspective on what's happening right now.

Part 4. Fall Guy! Don't Be the Canary in the Coal Mine!

Learning to be people-wise. Don't be the canary in the coal-mine. You're unlikely to have heard such an expression. This comes from the past. In the old days, miners who were afraid of poison gas in a new part of the mine, or after an explosion, would send a canary (little yellow singing bird) into the mine.

If he returned, then it was safe to enter the mine. If it did not return, then it was still too deadly to venture into the mine. It had to be ventilated further or simply wait for the poisonous gases to dissipate.

So, what do I mean by this? Many times, a group of kids or teens will have an idea for some daredevil plan or some prank that they know is a bit risky, either because it is dangerous, or because they're likely to get caught.

So, they usually devise to ask someone that they think will accept to do it, to be the first to try it. Who's that someone? Someone who is not popular but would really like to be. Someone who might be too afraid to refuse if a lot of kids are putting pressure on them. Someone who is flattered to be included in the plot. Someone who wants to show that they're brave and will try anything. I think that covers most of us.

When we are young, we are often not people-wise. It takes a couple of times of getting used and burned to learn. Where do you fit in this? It's important to be honest when thinking about yourself. Did you ever fall for such a scheme?

I know I did. I was naïve. I was shy and no one really paid attention to me. I was so flattered to be asked to lead the class in a prank on the teacher that I agreed right away even though I would never have ventured to do it on my own. Fortunately, not much happened. No one ratted on me when we were caught, so we were all punished…

Part 5. Dealing with Social Pressure

There are many kinds of social pressures. People frequently want to use others to satisfy their needs at others' expense.

Exercise 1: It can be one on one.

"Come with me to the store and you watch while I lift a couple of things."

"Help me out on the next test. You're such a good student! Just lean to the side so I can see your answers. Or, just text them to me."

"Just let me copy your homework; I'll be your friend."

Do you recognize any of those requests? Has this happened to you?

_____

_____

These are common. They happen to just about everyone.

Where do you want to stand?

_____

_____

Do you want to protect yourself from unwanted requests and possible consequences?

_____

_____

Do you believe you won't get caught?

_____

_____

Do you want to please people because you don't have enough friends?

_____

_____

Do you believe they will befriend you?

_____

_____

Do you want that kind of friend, one that you must buy?

_____

_____

Exercise 2: Can you give some examples of when you experienced social pressure?

1. _____

_____

2. _____

_____

3. _____

_____

Exercise 3: It is often several teens on one.

"Join us. We're going to smoke behind the gym." Or, "Be the watch while we smoke."

"Come to the party. There will be booze and weed. Don't tell anyone. Bring some booze from your house (they want you to steal it). Also, they want to make sure to get some. You might be the only one bringing it."

"We're all going to jump off the bridge into the river. It'll be fun. Kids do it all the time!" You're flattered that you've been asked. When you get there, they want you to go first. They'll dare you and goad you into trying it. They don't know if it is safe: you're the guinea pig. What do you do?

Have you ever been pressured by a group of teens or young adults to do something that you knew was wrong, illegal, or dangerous?

Can you give an example?

What happened? What did you do?

_____

_____

Why did you do it?

_____

_____

What was the outcome?

_____

_____

How did you feel about it?

_____

_____

Example: In a sad movie, the boy gives in to the pressure to be the first one to jump off a bridge, not daring to look cowardly. As a result, he breaks his neck in the shallow water and almost dies. After weeks in the hospital, he remains crippled and in a wheelchair. The other boys are so ashamed at first that they don't even go visit him: they are afraid of punishment or retaliation. But the hurt boy is bigger than that, recognizes his responsibility for his act, and invites them.

Example: In another movie, two boys want a third one to help them break into the school computer so that they can change their own grades. They assure him that it's fool-proof, no one will know. He hesitates. It's hard to say "no." He knows it's wrong. It puts his future college career at risk if he gets caught. There is nothing in there for him but risk as he has good grades. How to say "no." He reminds his friends of the risk to themselves if they get caught. He does end up refusing to help them but tells them how to do it. He ends up going one step further to protect them: he later goes into the system by himself and changes the boys' grades back to what they were originally. It's better to have a bad grade than to risk handicapping your future by getting caught.

Workbook for the Middle Teen Years

In the middle teenage years, you become much more aware of who you are, what you do, and how you do it. You are more able to think before you act and you are paying attention to making decisions, big and small, about your life. Here, you'll identify the different of your life. In the next chapters, you'll go into much more detail about how to manage your life.

Part 1. Thinking About Your Future

Exercise 1: What are your goals for your grades or schooling?

a. _____

b. _____

c. _____

d. _____

Exercise 2: What are your career/trade/work thoughts?

e. _____

f. _____

g. _____

h. _____

Part 2. Thinking About Your Relationships

Exercise 1: Relationships with parents or caregivers

Do you accept discipline? _____

_____

Do you respect the rules? _____

_____

Do you manage chores? _____

_____

Exercise 2: Relationships with siblings

How do you manage conflicts?

_____

_____

Do you respect others?

_____

_____

Do you provide guidance/support to brothers and sisters?

_____

_____

Are you generous or do you keep to yourself?

_____

_____

Exercise 3: How do you get along with peers?

Do you like to compete? _____

Do you prefer cliques? _____

Are you a loner? _____

Are you popular? _____

Exercise 4: How do you get along with friends?

Do you pick your friends well? _____

_____

Are you a good friend to others? _____

_____

Do you speak your mind in your relationships? _____

_____

Are you honest about what you want? _____

_____

Do you avoid being talked into doing things? _____

_____

Exercise 5: How do you get along with romantic partners?

Do you choose to date? _____

_____

Do you make decisions about your sexual involvement? _____

_____

If you are sexually active, are you staying safe?_____

_____

Are you keeping your goals, your future, in mind? _____

_____

Do you avoid pressure to make decisions? _____

_____

Are you clear with your partner about what you want? _____

_____

Do you stand by your decisions or give in to pressure? _____

_____

Do you acknowledge their wants as well as yours? _____

_____

Do you make decisions that fit you? _____

_____

Part 3. Section on Gender Identity/Sexual Orientation

The teen years are also a period of great physical and emotional changes as the young person develops sexual characteristics and maturity. This is a period with a lot of turmoil. I don't have to tell you about that!

For all youth, it is a period of discovering and, hopefully, acknowledging gender and sexual identity. While many teens feel comfortable in their gender, not all do. Also, while most teens are attracted to persons of the other sex, again, not all of them are.

Thus, for some teens, this is a period of particularly acute turmoil as they now perceive their identity to be different from the mainstream. Fortunately, today, it is becoming easier to acknowledge differences as some of the social taboos are disappearing. Still, it is a challenging time for many youths.

It is even hard to create a worksheet/questionnaire for this section. I wish for teens to be honest and be open with their truths. However, their truths are not always so clear to them. They may be difficult to acknowledge. In addition, teens and young adults need to be careful about sharing their truth with others.

So, if it makes sense for you to respond to these questions, please do so. However, if you won't, that's totally ok. This is about what you need for yourself.

Here are some definitions that might be useful:

Sex/Gender: the biological identity you are born with

Sexuality/sexual orientation: whom you are attracted to

Androgynous: appearing both male and female; unclear gender

Non-Binary: persons who cannot identify as either gender; they feel the need for an identity that encompasses more than a single gender.

Trans/Transsexual: persons who feel that their identity is different from their biological sex and decide to live with the gender that fits them (sometimes with sex-change surgery).

What is your Gender Identity? In our day, the terms for different aspects of gender identity and sexual orientation are being frequently added to. I will try to be current but please feel free to add those terms that feel comfortable for you. Only you know yourself.

Exercise 1: Gender Identity: I'll share mine here: Female (she/her/hers). Please circle the term(s) that apply to you.

Male Female Non-Binary Androgynous Unsure Queer Questioning Asexual

Two-Spirit Intersex Trans to Female Trans to Male

What are Your Pronouns: he/him/his she, her/hers they, them, their

Exercise 2: What is your Sexual Orientation? Please feel free to add your own answer.

Heterosexual Homosexual Bi-Sexual Pan Sexual Poly Amorous Asexual

Exercise 3: Have you shared your truth with anyone or are you keeping it private? Please choose from the following or add your own choice:

No one   Parents/Caregivers   Siblings   Friends   Counselors   Therapists   Support Groups

_____

Exercise 4: Who is offering support, helping you? Feel free to add as needed.

No one   Parents/Caregivers   Siblings   Friends   Counselors   Therapists   Support Groups

_____

Exercise 5: Are you being shunned or being discriminated against for your personal status?

Parents/Caregivers   Siblings   Friends   Classmates   Church   Work

_____

Exercise 6: What have you tried to get needed support?

_____

_____

Did you get the support you needed?

_____

_____

Exercise 7: How are you feeling currently? Do you need help? Is it urgent? What will you do?

I am feeling: poorly   scared   unhappy   barely ok   okay   well   very well

_____

_____

_____

You know this is a workbook. It can help you look at yourself, but you are the one who needs to get the help you need. Only you know whom you can go to in your family, among your friends.

Do you know how to find a counselor at school, through your parents or caregivers, maybe through a community agency, a support group, an emergency room if you are worried for your safety.

There are many places to get help and it is your responsibility to get it. It is for your well-being, your life, your future.

Workbook for the Late Teen/Young Adult Years

As you enter the late teen years and become a young adult, you are growing into the adult/person you want to become. Hopefully, you are engaged in pursuing goals to make your dreams a reality. You are becoming aware of pitfalls and temptations that distract you from your goals.

You are aware of your strengths and weaknesses and are developing skills to manage your behavior and your choices. You're learning to think things through carefully and make choices that fit your goals.

You're learning to choose friends that suit you and to avoid unhealthy peer pressure. You're learning to recognize whom you can trust and when to be cautious with people who may harm you in some way. This helps you feel empowered to win at life as you plan to engage in the adult life ahead of you.

That all sounds too good to be true! How could you get to feel like that? This book has been helping you prepare to feel like that!

Earlier in this chapter, you reviewed the basic skills you needed and were encouraged to practice them to succeed during the upcoming years. The following chapters are here to help you learn necessary skills and hone them until you feel empowered to manage your life the way you want it to be.

As you work your way through the following chapters, you will acquire the skills you need to become a responsible adult. You will come to feel empowered to choose the life you want to lead. You can become one of the successful people. It's up to you. Go for the prize!

CHAPTER 4

Get to Know Yourself: Find Your Strengths and Forge Ahead

Getting to know yourself

Introduction

In Chapters 1 and 2, you took a first close look at yourself and your development during childhood. Chapter 3 provided you with an overview of the skills you need to develop during your pre-teen and teen years as you grow from dependence to independence. Now, this chapter and those that follow will provide greater detail to help you acquire the skills you need for your successful entry into adulthood.

You have already filled out other questionnaires, stating facts about you. Maybe you've also used the Identity Scale and the Behavior Scale. Those are important aspects of your identity, and they are the ones that you will be looking at most closely.

Looking at yourself honestly and identifying your strengths and your weaknesses is essential in learning to manage your life. With self-awareness, you can make better choices for yourself as you seek to identify your goals and find your direction.

As you grow into your teen years, growing more separate from parents and caretakers is essential. As you begin to do this, you become more aware of your needs and the way you want to live your life.

Later in this chapter, you'll learn to use Decision Trees to map out your choices with an eye on their outcomes. You'll be able to see into the future, your future.

The Importance of Being Honest and Avoiding Self-Judgment

It's important to know yourself. If you are not truthful with yourself, then you can't know yourself and help yourself become the person you want to be.

It's important to accept yourself <u>without judgment</u>. When I am working with someone and I tell them they are not being judged, it's a big relief for them. Then, they can acknowledge bad feelings, embarrassment, regret, or even shame. We all have those feelings and it is important to avoid judging ourselves.

Accepting yourself without judgment is the best way you can work towards the future. Otherwise, the judgment and the negative feelings get in your way, keep you from moving forward, and make you feel hopeless about reaching your goals.

When we face our truth, we can know ourselves and start to choose what we want for ourselves. We can choose to make it happen.

Part 1. Finding Your Strengths. Recognizing Your Qualities

On the Identity Scale, it is important to mark not only where you are now, but where you want to be, your goal for yourself. It also shows your direction, your path to your future. It is important to be honest with yourself on this scale. Otherwise, it is not useful to you.

Exercise 1: Looking at the scale, name five qualities that you are happy with now:

_____

_____

_____

_____

_____

Exercise 2: Then, name five qualities you want to improve:

_____

_____

_____

_____

_____

Part 2. Acknowledging Your Behaviors

On the Behavior Scale, you again need to identify where you are now (honestly) and where you want to be in the future. These are goals and you can start working on them immediately. Most likely, you've already been working on them.

Exercise 1: Name five behaviors that make you happy with yourself:

_____

_____

_____

_____

_____

Exercise 2: Name five behaviors you want to improve on:

_____

_____

_____

_____

_____

Part 3. Using Your Strengths to Manage Your Weaknesses

We all have strengths and weaknesses. Strengths are extremely useful: they can help you improve your weaknesses. Weaknesses are opportunities for growth, for building a better future for yourself. Often, weaknesses that are corrected become great strengths.

Exercise:

Can you match 5 strengths with 5 weaknesses and see how the strengths will help you overcome the weaknesses?

Example: Courage can help overcome shyness. Ambitiousness helps overcome pessimism.

_____

_____

_____

_____

_____

Part 4. Forging Ahead: The Importance of Separation

As teens get older, they begin to feel separate from parents or other caregivers. They want to run their own lives. That's natural and healthy but it can't happen overnight. Parents and caregivers need to evaluate how much freedom to give their teens to foster responsibility for their choices. Parents/caregivers need to have behavior guidelines in their house and teens are expected to abide by them. There needs to be clear rules and clear penalties for not obeying the rules.

Exercise 1: What are the rules in your home? Are there clear rules? Are there clear penalties?

Rule about curfew

Rule: _____

Penalty: _____

Rule about having friends over

Rule: _____

Penalty: _____

Rule about using the car

Rule: _____

Penalty: _____

Rule about doing homework

Rule: _____

Penalty: _____

Rule about attending school

Rule: _____

Penalty: _____

Rule about smoking, alcohol, drug use

Rule: _____

Penalty: _____

Rule about phone use

Rule: _____

Penalty: _____

Rule about computer/video games

Rule: _____

Penalty: _____

Rule about hitting or hurting siblings

Rule: _____

Penalty: _____

Rule about chores

Rule: _____

Penalty: _____

Rule about pet care

Rule: _____

Penalty: _____

Rule about mealtime

Rule: _____

Penalty: _____

Rule about going into others' rooms, using others' things.

Rule: _____

Penalty: _____

Rule about respecting adults/siblings

Rule: _____

Penalty: _____

Exercise 2: Now, suppose that there aren't clear rules in your home. Look at these again and check which ones you would need to have in place to feel things were under control. Listen to your voice that tells you your best path. Be honest with yourself. Remember, these are private: they do not have to be shared unless you want to share.

Identify the rules you would need and what the consequences of violating them would be, to keep you safe on your path.

Rule about curfew

Rule: _____

Penalty: _____

Rule about having friends over

Rule: _____

Penalty: _____

Rule about using the car

Rule: _____

Penalty: _____

Rule about doing homework

Rule: _____

Penalty: _____

Rule about attending school

Rule: _____

Penalty: _____

Rule about smoking, alcohol, drug use

Rule: _____

Penalty: _____

Rule about phone use

Rule: _____

Penalty: _____

Rule about computer/video games

Rule: _____

Penalty: _____

Rule about hitting or hurting siblings

Rule: _____

Penalty: _____

Rule about chores

Rule: _____

Penalty: _____

Rule about pet care

Rule: _____

Penalty: _____

Rule about mealtime

Rule: _____

Penalty: _____

Rule about going into others' rooms, using others' things.

Rule: _____

Penalty: _____

Rule about respecting adults/siblings

Rule: _____

Penalty: _____

Part 5. Making Better Choices with Decision Trees

This is a good place to learn about decision-making. This is an important skill, useful not just during your teen and young adult years, but throughout your whole life. For this purpose, I have decided to use Decision Trees to promote decision-making with insight and foresight.

Decision Trees offer a way of mapping out your choices and their outcome (consequences) when you are trying to decide. It can be an easy decision or a difficult one, a simple one or a complex one. You can use Decision Trees to "see into the future" as you map out different options and outcomes.

You can even use them for things that are past. This is particularly useful when you are faced with a poor outcome and would like to figure out what happened, where you went wrong, how you could have chosen otherwise.

To use a Decision Tree, you need to start with a choice to make or even a dilemma, a difficult choice. It is also best if you have an actual goal in mind because Decision Trees are particularly helpful in keeping your goals in mind. The challenge is that you often have many competing goals, some are short term goals, some are longer term goals, or even lifelong goals.

Luis' Decision Tree

Luis has one main goal in mind: to pass math class because he wants to be an engineer, like his father. Luis tends to be hungry and tired or distracted in math class which is right before lunch break. Luis has been told that he should have breakfast to avoid this problem. He doesn't really believe that having breakfast will make a difference. However, Luis is willing to try it out and experiment with different breakfasts since he wants to avoid after-school tutorials.

This is also a goal because he wants to get an after-school job to make some money. He is considering his options and what would work best for him. Follow the branches and you will see how each choice leads to an outcome.

You can see here that Luis must build a ladder of choices to lead him to his goal of paying attention in class. We could take it further and include whether he still needs after-school help, or even if he is able to get a job after school. But here we just focus on whether he can manage well in math class.

Exercise: Put the following steps in the right order so that Luis can go from the main question to the second, then third, then reach goal.

1. eat a healthy breakfast?

2. paying attention in class?

3. have breakfast?

4. Is he hungry?

Answer: 3, 1, 4, 2 is the sequence needed here as you go from main decision to goal.

What choices are most likely to get Luis to his goal? If you look at the Decision Tree for Luis in Chapter 1, Part 6, you will be able to follow the steps that lead Luis to reach his goal.

Part 6. Building a Decision Tree

Now let me show you how to go about building a Decision Tree. It seems complicated, but you'll soon get the hang of it.

First and most important is to state the decision as a choice between Yes or No. Then you take the Yes branch and ask the next question as a choice. With each answer, you ask the next question as a choice. Sometimes, the tree branches have fewer levels, sometimes more.

Here is an example where you will choose the question (that's the hardest part).

Let's build it now. Take a blank Decision Tree sheet so that you can see it and fill in the answers as we move forward. It is much easier to understand it you are filling it in as we go. Follow the link to the video in the available tools on the Readers Page, at www.iwanttobeme.org.

My wish: To go see my granddaughter next month.

My decision: At the time of writing this exercise, I am trying to decide whether to go see my granddaughter in a month. I would need to fly, rent a car, and stay at a hotel. It's expensive and I am not sure I can afford it.

I don't even know if I can take the time off from work. I worry that I might end up being short on rent. So, these three things need to go into my decision process. I also need to consider that if I don't go now, there may be other chances. So, it's not necessarily the last chance.

Exercise 1: Choose the MAIN question to start the tree:

Do I make the trip now?

When will I go see her?

Does she want me to visit?

Can I get a good flight?

Answer: The MAIN question is: Do I make the trip now?

Next, let's work with the YES Branch

Exercise 2: Choose the next question on the YES branch:

Can I spend the money?

Will it make me late on the rent?

What if I get evicted?

Should I ask a friend to lend me money?

Answer: Can I spend the money/afford the trip?

Exercise 3: Again, let's take the YES branch first.

Choose the next question on the YES branch:

Are there cheap flights?

Can I get time off when I need it?

Should I wait until I have the money?

Where is the best place to stay?

Answer: Can I get time off? If it leads to YES – I can go. No problem.

If it leads to NO – I can't go now, maybe later.

Exercise 4: Now choose the NO answer to "can I afford it?"

Will I be short on rent?

Should I borrow the money?

Should I wait until I can afford it?

Can I find a cheaper way to go?

Answer: Since I don't like to borrow money, the question is: Will I be short on rent?

Exercise 5: Now follow the Yes answer and see if you can work around it:

Will I get evicted (terrible consequence)?

Can I delay the rent payment?

Will I have to pay a late fee? How much?

Can I borrow the money to complete the rent?

Answer: Let's pick the worst case possible: Will I get evicted?

It might be a YES. Maybe I am already 3 months behind on the rent

Lastly, follow to the NO answer: Here it is important to consider consequences of doing something I can't really afford because I still must pay the rent.

Exercise 6: Will it get me into more debt than I can manage?

I will put it on a credit card and worry about it later

I can delay paying the rent with no problem

I will borrow the money to complete the rent

I should get overtime pay at work

Answer: Can I delay paying the rent with no problem?

* * *

Now, let's look at the NO branch of the MAIN question. If I decide not to go, for whatever reason.

Well, that's sad and frustrating. Could I have other choices/options?

Exercise 7: What is the next question?

> Are there other options?
>
> Can I hope to go sometime?
>
> How can I make it happen?
>
> Should I just give up?

Answer: Are there other options?

Go to the YES branch:

> What are the choices for me?
>
> Save money till I can go?
>
> Get an extra job to get more money?
>
> Do overtime to get more money?
>
> Borrow from a friend?

Answer: Save money till I can go.

Go to the NO answer: none of these will work because I am not good at managing and saving money. This is an important realization that would encourage me to get good at it.

Go to the YES branch: try to get there in 3 months.

Exercise 8: If I have concluded that there are no other choices, I could explore my choices a little further

Go to the NO answer:

> Is it really the only chance to take that trip?

Go to the NO box

> Maybe there will be other trips in the future.

Go to the YES box: I could find things to do instead:

> Skype or FaceTime with my granddaughter.

Dr. B's Decision Tree

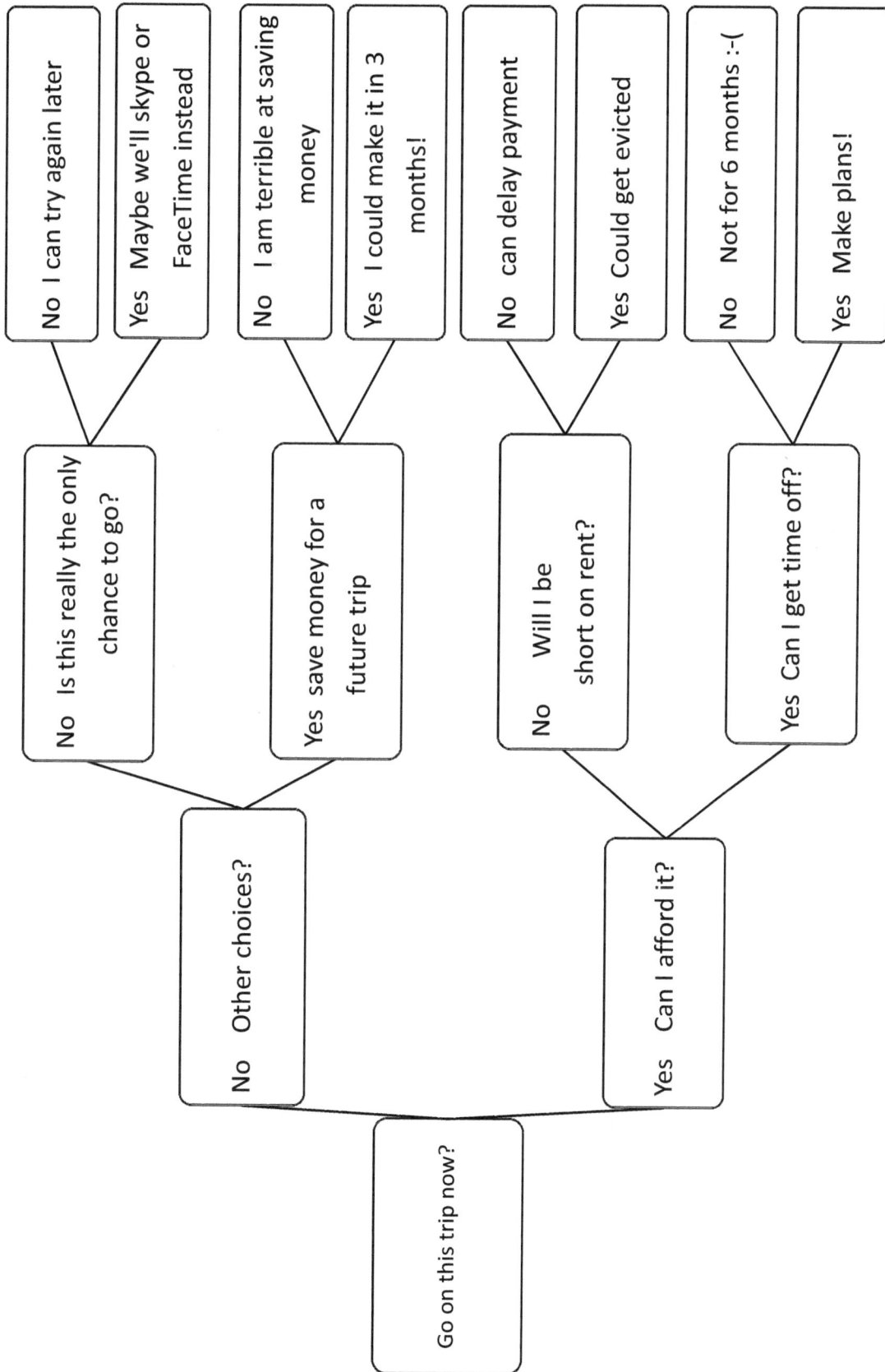

No I can try again later

Yes Maybe we'll skype or FaceTime instead

No I am terrible at saving money

Yes I could make it in 3 months!

No can delay payment

Yes Could get evicted

No Not for 6 months :-(

Yes Make plans!

No Is this really the only chance to go?

Yes save money for a future trip

No Will I be short on rent?

Yes Can I get time off?

No Other choices?

Yes Can I afford it?

Go on this trip now?

Part 7. You Build a Decision Tree

Now you build a decision tree for a choice that you need to make.

What is your goal?

_____

What steps will you need to take to reach your goal?

     Step 1. _____

     Step 2. _____

     Step 3. _____

     Step 4. _____

What choices will you encounter as you choose your path?

Down the YES path:

    1.   First YES box _____

    2.   Second YES box _____

    3.   Second NO box _____

Down the NO path

    4.   First No box _____

    5.   Second YES box _____

    6.   Second No box _____

The fourth column lets you list the outcomes of all the choices. Sometimes, as you have seen in this book, the outcomes are already available in the third column. That is ok. What is important is that you follow the paths to their conclusions.

Build your tree and fill in the YES and NO answers in the blank tree on the next page (or get blank form from website: www.iwanttobeme.org Readers Page, code:bisdt2017).

Your Decision Tree

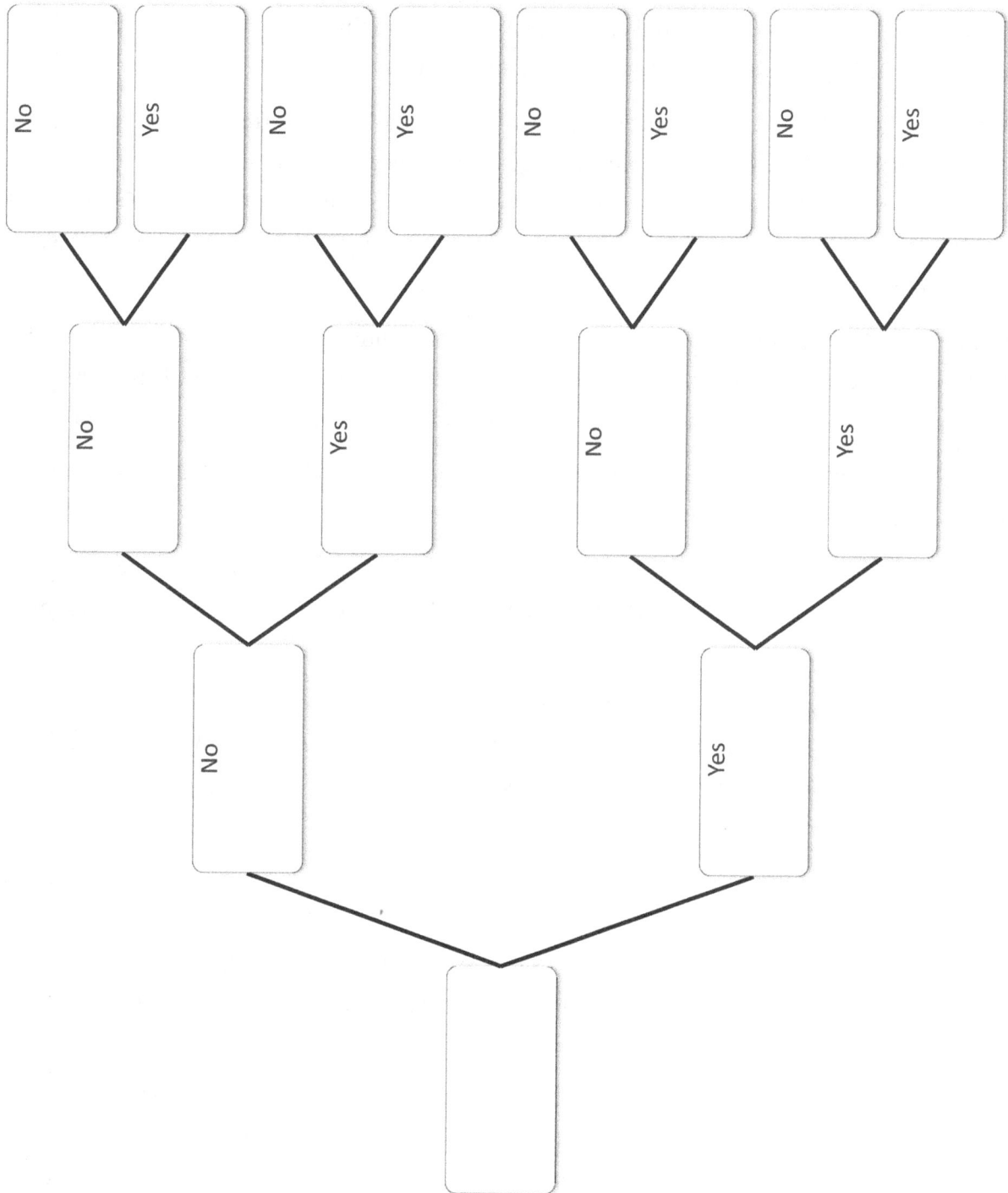

No	Yes	No	Yes	No	Yes	No	Yes

No	Yes	No	Yes

No	Yes

Part 8. Decision Tree with Competing Goals – a Dilemma

Introduction: With Luis, we looked at a situation where all the goals were lined up. Luis wanted to do better in math class and avoid after school tutorials, so that he could get a job after school. Eventually, he hopes to be good enough to become an engineer.

We're now going to look at Sha'anice's dilemma. (Sha'anice's Decision Tree in Chapter 1, Part 6). That's a decision where there are competing goals. Sha'anice wants to go to a party even if she must lie to her mother about it, but she also wants to do well on a test to avoid having to go to summer school. How do you decide when you have competing goals? This happens all the time, so it is important to weigh the choices and their consequences.

Sha'anice really wants to do both things; she focuses on an immediate, emotional goal (have fun, be popular) and a more distant, objective goal (the next test that will determine whether she passes the course). Sha'anice really wishes that they weren't both happening at the same time, but they are.

How does she examine her choices and their consequences at each step in the decision-making process?

a. Sha'anice must think about what may happen at the party, whether there might be drugs and alcohol, whether she might make poor decisions, whether they all might get into trouble.

b. Finally, she needs to think whether she will be able to study enough to do well on the test. She must look at alternative choices, whether she will study with a friend or just socialize and watch movies, whether she will have the discipline to study and do well on the test.

This decision shows why it is so important to know your strengths and weaknesses. For example, if you spend time with a friend, will you study together, or will you just make it a social time? This happens to all of us. It happens all the time. We always need to weigh our long-term goals against our immediate needs for satisfaction. How strong is our will to take care of ourselves for the long run, not just the immediate moment?

If you go to a party where there is alcohol and drugs, will you take care of yourself by leaving? Will you keep from engaging in those dangerous behaviors? Will you make sure you're safe from people who are drinking and smoking weed, doing drugs? We hear about so many people who end up using and getting raped. It does happen. It doesn't take too much alcohol for a teen to do things they wouldn't do otherwise.

You can see that life gets complicated very quickly when you are a teen. Suddenly, there is no one to make decisions for you. Of course, your parents or caregivers will hopefully have taught you to take care of yourself, to look out for yourself, to keep your priorities squarely in front of you. But now that's your job. You must decide what is important to you, what is more important when there are conflicting goals.

Sometimes, it is good if you can decide ahead of time. That way, the challenge will be to remember your earlier decision rather than having to decide on the spot. It is important to decide what you will do and what you won't do.

Look at what Sha'anice needs to decide. What are the chances Sha'anice will do well on the test if she goes to the party? If she spends the evening studying with a friend?

Now follow her path on the decision tree. As mentioned in the book, if Sha'anice knew herself well, she could study enough to be on track to passing first and go to the party later. She would have to decide to stay sober at the party to take care of herself during the party and not suffer a hangover the next day. (Review Sha'anice Decision Tree in Chapter 1, Part 6).

Part 9. Building a Decision Tree to Review a Past Experience

Introduction: Now let's look at a decision that you made where things didn't turn out as expected. (use the blank Decision Tree on the next page). Can you identify your goal or competing goals?

Main goal: _____

Is there a competing goal: _____

Can you identify the questions at each stage of the decision?

1. _____

2. _____

3. _____

4. _____

Can you see where you didn't know yourself well enough to control for the wanted outcome?

Did you hear your inner voice when you took that "wrong" turn away from your goals? YES NO

That inner voice could have guided you. It is important to listen to it. It is the voice that takes care of you.

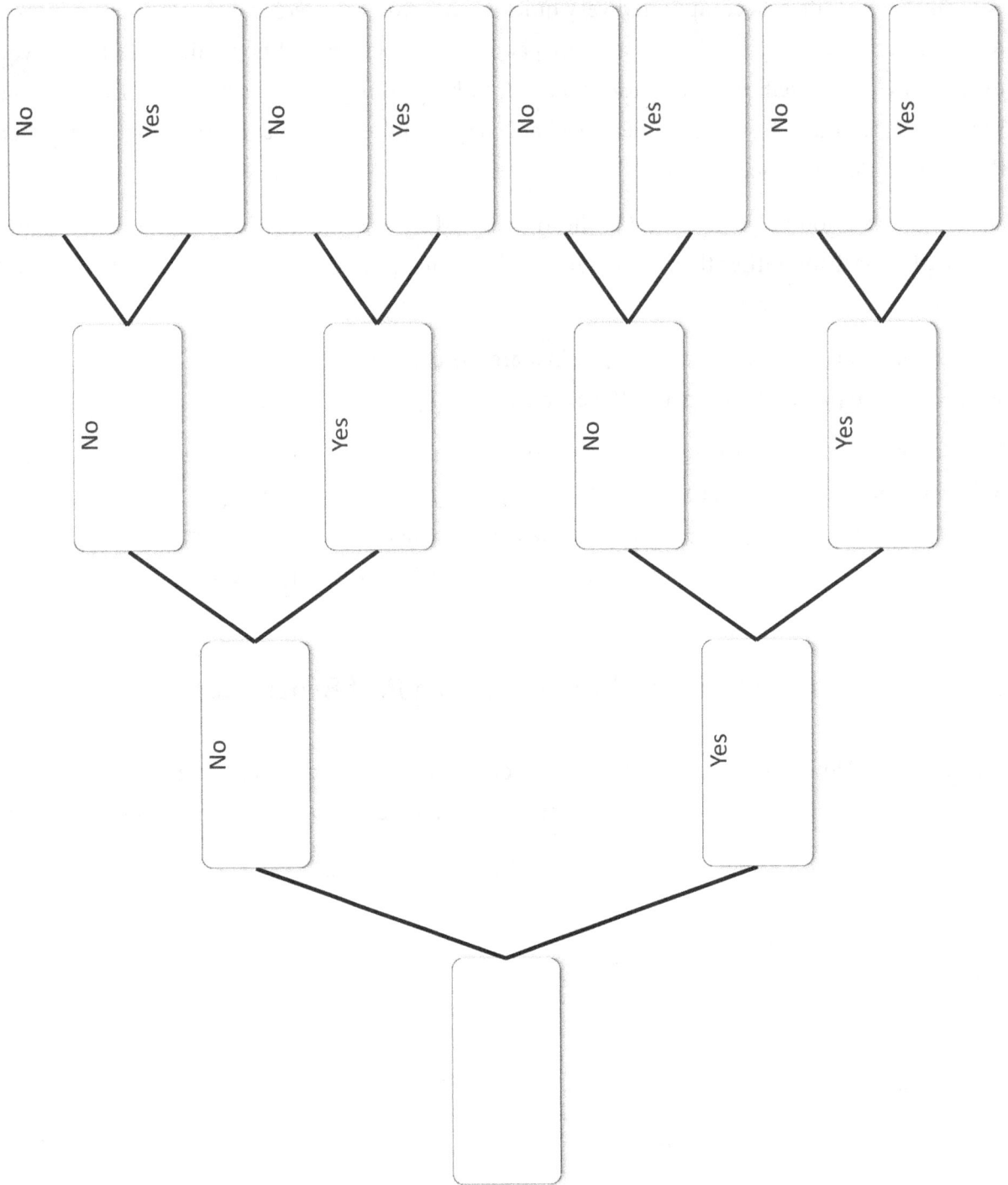

No	Yes	No	Yes	No	Yes	No	Yes

No	Yes	No	Yes

No	Yes

Part 10. Decision Tree for a Difficult and Important Decision

Introduction: Now, let's look at Cameron's situation. (Cameron's Decision Tree in Chapter 1, Part 6). This is a situation when there is peer pressure and it comes from someone that's significant to Cameron. Cameron has a new partner who is eager to have sex. Cameron is not ready but may be afraid of losing partner.

This is a common situation and I recommend that you put yourself in Cameron's shoes and think about your decision ahead of time. It might still be difficult to make the decision when you're with someone special, but it will help if you know what you want ahead of time. This is a big decision that can have large consequences for you and your partner. So, think about it carefully.

Of course, the easiest way to get out of difficult situations is to avoid them altogether. Cameron could make his/her choice clear to his/her partner as they enter in a relationship. Cameron could also avoid intimacy if he or she is not ready for it.

Conclusion:

In all these exercises, you can see how important it is to know yourself, to listen to your inner voice, to use your strengths and to acknowledge your weaknesses, as you choose the life you want to lead.

CHAPTER 5

Learn to Live with Your Emotions: Manage Your Behavior

EMOTIONS

This chapter is about your emotions and your behavior. How do they fit together? How do you take charge of both your emotions and your behavior? You started looking at this in chapter 3, but we'll look at it more closely now. Here, you will go beyond awareness to managing your emotions and behavior.

This is the biggest challenge of not only the teen years, but all our lives. The better we do this, the more successful we can become. Therefore, there is a whole chapter devoted to learning to manage this challenge.

Part 1. Understanding Emotions

Let's start with emotions. EMOTIONS ARE NATURAL AND NORMAL. They are necessary as they tell us how we feel about what is happening to us or to others around us. They can be strong and overwhelming: both the negative ones, like fear and anger, and the positive emotions, like joy and pleasure.

Have you ever screamed when frightened? Have you gotten angry when someone was mean to you? Have you ever cried when you were moved by something wonderful? All those reactions are natural.

It is important to recognize, acknowledge, and then accept our emotions. They are essential. However, it is also most important to choose how we are going to act in response to our emotions.

It is important to recognize what you are feeling, to label it, to acknowledge it.

It is important to accept your feelings.

It is important to avoid shutting your feelings down, shoving them out of your consciousness.

95

It is also important to avoid simply reacting to your feelings.

It is important to separate your feelings from your behaviors.

It is important to avoid reacting to your feelings with unwanted behaviors.

It is important to decide on your behavior, choose your actions.

Part 2. Recognizing Emotions

How do you acknowledge your anger? Do you feel it in your hands, the pit of your stomach, the hairs on your neck rising?

How do you acknowledge sadness? Do you cry? Do you get a lump in your throat? Do you deny sadness?

How do you acknowledge fear? Do you freeze when afraid? Do you get angry or even enraged when afraid? Do you run or hide? Do you fake being not afraid? Do you get ready to fight?

How do you acknowledge joy or happiness? Do you relax? Do you laugh or smile? Do you feel anxious because you're not used to that feeling? Do you get tearful? Do you hide your mouth with your hands, as if you were going to scream?

How do you acknowledge excitement? Do you jump up and down? Do you fidget? Do you run around? Do you cover your mouth with your hands?

How do you acknowledge anxiety or worry? Do you feel tightness in your body? Where? Do you feel afraid? Do you try to ignore the anxiety? Do you want to push it down, out of mind?

Exercise: Now, identify how you experience the following emotions:

1. Pleasure

   _____

   _____

2. Excitement

   _____

   _____

3. Joy

_____

_____

4. Anger

_____

_____

5. Fear

_____

_____

6. Sadness

_____

_____

7. Anxiety/worry

_____

_____

Part 3. Living with Negative Emotions

Remember that there are many reasons to experience fear and anger. Some of these were explored in Chapter 3. It often takes a long time to learn to manage those feelings. In this chapter, we start by acknowledging them and helping ourselves cope and heal.

The need for self-soothing. Self-soothing is about taking care of ourselves after a strong or negative emotion.

We may feel overwhelmed.

We may be fighting our first response.

We may need a little time to ourselves.

Sometimes a few seconds are enough to re-rout from a reaction and choose how to act.

Sometimes, we react right away and then regret our behavior.

Other times, we take the time to stay in control, but we are still hurting and needing recovery time.

So, what do we do to recover?

Most of us like to have some privacy to recover.

Some people like to go for a walk outdoors.

Some go to a separate room, listen to music, read something, watch tv to take their mind off the pain.

Some people keep a journal of what is happening to them.

Whatever you like to do, it is important to take care of yourself and be kind to yourself.

If you don't have ways to recover, it is important to find ways. So, here you may list things that you already do as well as things that you want to try.

Exercise 1: What do you like to do when you need recovery time from emotional overwhelm?

1. _____

   _____

2. _____

   _____

3. _____

   _____

4. _____

   _____

Exercise 2: What are some things you'd like to try when you need recovery time?

1. _____

   _____

2. _____

   _____

Conclusion: it is important to become comfortable with emotions, to acknowledge them, experience them, and accept them as an important part of your life and experience. But this chapter is also about managing your behavior.

Part 4. Separating Emotions from Behavior

Introduction: Most people think of behavior as an automatic response to emotions. Most people therefore think that they must manage the emotions. We CAN'T manage emotions…but we CAN manage our behavior. Emotions and Behavior are separate.

1. We experience our emotions and we choose our behaviors. However, that is something we must learn. When we are little we must learn to accept the NO of our parents or other caregivers, even if we are upset about it. We learn to manage our behavior. We learn to obey rules and orders even when we don't like them. So, we have already learned some ways to manage our behavior.

2. As we grow towards adulthood, we come to realize that this is the MOST IMPORTANT skill to learn.

   a. We don't want to allow others to push our buttons and make us react in ways we don't really want. WE WANT TO BE IN CHARGE OF OURSELVES.

   b. We don't want others to intimidate or frighten us. We want to stand our ground, meet our goals.

   c. We don't want others to manipulate us into doing their bidding, sometimes with flattery, compliments, or even threats. We want and need to be our own masters.

Conclusion

And yet, we know that we often just react to emotions, without taking the time to identify them, acknowledge them, and sit with them. We don't take the time to take care of ourselves and soothe negative feelings. Often, there are negative consequences. In addition, we often feel that we weren't true to ourselves, that we lost control of our decision process, our free will.

Behavior

Part 5. Managing Behavior

So, how do you keep from reacting to your emotions? How do you become your own master? How do you choose your behavior and feel powerful, in charge of your life?

1. One of the oldest tricks is to Count to Ten. This gives you the time to pull back and then decide what you want to do. In the movies, the person often turns away from their opponent to take time to recover and then strike back. I don't think I want to encourage you to strike someone as that is not a solution and it often leads to more problems. We call that escalation.

2. What I encourage you to do is consider choices and consequences. What would be most effective at that moment?

Exercise 1: Let's pick something that happens often in the school yard. Someone you dislike comes up to you and starts pushing your buttons, saying things just to provoke you to a fight (which will get you both in trouble). So, of course, you are feeling challenged, angry, maybe even intimidated, hesitant, or ready to hit him. What do you do?

a. You say nothing and try to ignore him

b. You walk away

c. You tell him to buzz off, leave you alone

d. You call him names and start yelling at him

e. You see him coming, expecting trouble, and leave the area

f. You laugh and turn your back, walk away

g. You stay silent for a moment, looking annoyed and bored

h. You shrug your shoulders and walk away

You may not believe it but all of these are actual possibilities. Remember: you don't have to engage with the other person. You are free to choose your behavior.

Exercise 2: Which of those would you like to try? Can you think of any other ways to respond, not react, but respond to a bully?

_____

_____

_____

_____

Now is a good time to look closely at how you handle situations, both comfortable and uncomfortable. It is, as usual, important to be honest and to avoid judging yourself.

Exercise 3 : Think of something uncomfortable that did happen to you. What did you feel and what did you do? Did you react or were you able to choose your behavior/your response?

a. What happened?

_____

_____

b. What did you do?

_____

_____

c. Did you react or did you choose your response?

_____

_____

d. Why? What were your goals then, what are your long-term goals?

_____

_____

e. What were the consequences? Were you satisfied with the outcome?

_____

_____

Exercise 4: "Do over" time: Now think back on the event and think about what were your options?

1. _____
2. _____
3. _____
4. _____

Exercise 5: What do you wish you had done? How could you have done it?

1. _____
2. _____
3. _____
4. _____

Exercise 6: What might you do next time? How would you do it? How would you feel about your behavior?

1. _____
2. _____
3. _____
4. _____

This exercise cannot be done too often or too many times. We all need to take charge of our behavior. This means being aware of what we do and why. It also means being willing to make the changes we need to be successful in our lives. (You can get blank forms from website: www.iwanttobeme.org Readers Page code:bisdt2017).

Part 6. Making Important Decisions Ahead of Time

There are important choices that you can think about and make ahead of time. Some of these include decisions about alcohol and drug use, sexual activities, maybe even lying and stealing. You might also decide about using weapons, threats, and force.

Exercise 1: Your decisions about alcohol and drug use. Name each one that concerns you:

_____

_____

_____

_____

Exercise 2: Your decisions about sexual behaviors and activities:

_____

_____

_____

_____

Exercise 3: Your decisions about lying, stealing, and maybe other behaviors you're concerned about:

_____

_____

_____

_____

Exercise 4: Your decisions about using weapons, threats, and force:

_____

_____

_____

_____

Conclusion

Of course, there is no time to pull out a blank Decision Tree when you are faced with a challenging situation, so it is a good thing to be aware of your dreams, your goals, your needs.

You can have decided ahead of time how you will respond to a situation because the situation has taken place before. You can have learned from previous negative consequences. That's how most of us learn: we learn not to touch hot things, not to run after our favorite ball into traffic, not to let others pick on us, not to give in to teasing and taunts.

When we have decided not to be vulnerable to negative encounters, we present in a different manner. It comes across as a signal to others. We tend to be left in peace. We don't even have to deal with negative encounters. We stand our ground. We are secure in ourselves.

Even if you didn't decide ahead of time on your response, you can think quickly. You can listen to what your inner voice or gut-feeling is telling you. Take a moment to remember your goals before you act. You need to remember to be yourself rather than what someone else wants you to be. Hide your buttons so that they can't be pushed!

But there is no magic. This is one of the most difficult things to learn and it takes a long time to master it. Some people never master it and cannot take charge of their life. I hope that you can struggle to master this priceless skill and take charge of your life as best as possible.

CHAPTER 6

Parenting Yourself: Learn to Be Your Own Guide

Becoming Your Own Good Parent

It is the work of the teen and young adult years to take over the work of our parents or caregivers and become our own guides. However, we must be careful to become our own GOOD parent.

Sometimes, our parents/caregivers are so eager to have us be our best that they criticize frequently and we feel that we're never good enough. This becomes part of how we see ourselves. This is common.

Sometimes, parents or caregivers are so distracted by their own needs that they are not present to our needs. That is tough because then it is easy not to attend to our own needs. Those don't seem to count anyway.

Sometimes, parents or caregivers are angry with their lives and they take it out on their children, becoming angry and even abusive, yelling at them, belittling them, even cursing, and threatening them, sometimes hurting them physically.

Sometimes, teens have already learned to belittle themselves, to engage in negative self-talk, putting themselves down, criticizing their performance, and feeling that they are just not good enough. When that happens, it is important to unlearn this kind of self-destructive talk and try to listen to your inner voice, to take good care of yourself.

Part 1. Become Your Own Good Parent

What are GOOD parents? What do GOOD parents do?

Good parents put your best interest first. They want the best for you.

Good parents will acknowledge and respect your feelings.

Good parents will guide you, show you how to recover when you are feeling hurt or angry.

Good parents don't give in to tantrums; they don't spoil you.

Good parents are supportive. They are always there for you; they have your back.

Good parents point out mistakes; teach you how to fix them if you need help.

Good parents compliment you on efforts and successes.

Good parents appreciate you as you are. They respect you for who you are.

Good parents will encourage you to solve your problems, and guide you as needed.

Good parents will help you "think back" and understand what went well or what went wrong.

Good parents have expectations of you that are realistic, that fit you.

Good parents have faith in you; they know that you are capable of success.

Good parents encourage you to try new things that are good for you even when you are afraid.

Good parents warn you about poor behavior choices; they are clear about boundaries.

Good parents are always there when you need them. You can count on them.

Good parents know when to say "no;" they know how to keep you safe.

OMG! You're probably thinking "That is so much work!" How am I ever going to be like that for myself (and one day for my children)? Well, let's remember that you have time. You have that whole second decade of life and more to become independent and responsible for yourself. The most important thing to remember is to be kind to yourself. This is where that inner voice, that little voice that whispers your need for safety, your need for good outcomes for yourself, comes in. It is the thing to pay close attention to.

Time to Begin the Work!

Part 2. What Does Your Good Parent Do?

Your good parent is that little voice that tells you who you are and what you need to be the best you, the You you'd love to be.

Your own good parent is that little voice that:

1. Is always there for you, has your back

2. Pays attention to what you are doing

3. Lets you know when you are doing something good

4. Lets you know when you are making a mistake

5. Encourages you to take care of yourself

6. Expects you to succeed

7. Expects you to make good choices

8. Forgives you your mistakes

9. Encourages you to try hard things

10. Helps you when you are afraid

11. Rejoices when you succeed

12. Praises you for effort

Exercise 1: How are you your own good parent?

What are 5 things you do for yourself that show that you are your own good parent?

1. _____

2. _____

3. _____

4. _____

5. _____

Exercise 2: What would you like to do for yourself, that you're not doing yet?

1. _____

2. _____

3. _____

4. _____

5. _____

Exercise 3: Are you able to hear your true voice, be your own good guide/parent? We all have that ability to hear ourselves, be true to ourselves, be our own great guide.

_____

_____

_____

Exercise 4: Sometimes, it is too hard. You can't to make the effort to listen to yourself and take care of your need: Can you think of an example when you didn't have the courage to follow your voice?

_____

_____

_____

Part 3. Sorting Out the Good Voice From the Negative Voice

Exercise 1: Sorting out the good voice from the negative voices:

Among the many comments below, pick the ones that are a good voice/your good parent. Circle the letter for each voice that has your back and cross out the letter for the ones that hit you over the head. It is not always easy.

- a. You did your best.
- b. You could have done better.
- c. You knew better than to do this.
- d. You put up a good effort.
- e. Next time, you'll know better.
- f. How could you know what would happen?
- g. That was a tough lesson to learn.
- h. You showed great courage.
- i. You took good care of yourself.
- j. You should not have done that.
- k. That was a poor choice.

l.   I am ashamed of you.

m. You always embarrass me.

n.   That sure turned out to be a mistake.

o.   What could you have done to change the situation?

p.   We all make mistakes sometimes. The important thing is to learn from them.

q.   What did you learn from this mishap?

r.   You were stupid to get involved with this.

s.   Was there a way you could have foreseen what would happen?

t.   Let that be a lesson to you. You'll be more careful next time.

u.   Everybody makes mistakes sometimes.

v.   You'd better get even with them, so they don't do it next time.

Exercise 2: Sometimes, the voice you hear is mean, self-defeating, refusing to believe in yourself: can you think of a time you were defeated by the mean, discouraging voice?

_____

_____

_____

_____

Exercise 3: Can you think of a time when you were able to overcome the self-defeating voice and were true to yourself?

_____

_____

_____

_____

Part 4. Getting Past the Mean, Self-Defeating Voice

Getting past the mean, self-defeating voice takes effort but it is always possible. There are many ways of reminding yourself that you can be true to yourself.

a.   You need to recognize the negative self-talk that puts you down.

b. You can identify your patterns and learn to put a stop to them.

c. You can remind yourself that it is not your true voice.

d. That voice was taught to you and you can unlearn it.

e. You need to believe that you also have a true voice, even if it is hidden.

f. You can open to hearing your true voice, your love for yourself.

g. You are a good person (even when you make mistakes).

h. You deserve the best for yourself – you can hear the good voice inside you.

i. You must take care of yourself for the future – make it the best you can.

j. Every time you do something good for yourself, your true voice grows stronger and it becomes easier to overcome any mean, or self-defeating voice.

k. You're the only one who can do this for yourself. Learning to put yourself first and taking care of yourself is the best thing you can do for yourself.

Here you will see how another teen handled his or her situation and you will be asked how you handled yours.

Manuel's being his own good parent

1. Manuel doesn't like to do homework and is not good at learning. He wants to do well in school, but he thinks it's too hard. Yesterday, he encouraged and challenged himself to try harder; he made the effort and did all his homework. Then, he did well in all his classes today because he was prepared.

   Manuel felt proud of himself, told himself that it was a good day and he had earned it with hard work. Manuel wanted to continue to take such good care of himself.

2. Manuel was mocked for participating in class today. Classmates called him a brown-nose, a nerd. Manuel was embarrassed and didn't know if he could keep up his effort. He likes to be popular.

   Manuel realized that he was hurt and angry with his classmates. He took some time after school to listen to his favorite music and started to feel better.

   Then, Manuel reminded himself that he had made a good effort for himself, for his future, for his dreams. That was wonderful. Manuel realized that others may be jealous of his success and resent him. That is painful for Manuel.

3. Manuel tried to think of his options:

Could he learn to ignore them and take care of himself? Could he help friends who are not doing as well? Offer to do homework with them? Show them the way?

Could he make other friends, with classmates who are working hard and wanting to succeed in school?

Your situation

1. Think of something good that you did for yourself today. It can be something small like you ate a good breakfast.

_____

_____

How did you acknowledge yourself? Praise? Did you feel good about it? Or did you forget to pat yourself on the back?

_____

_____

2. Think of something unpleasant that happened in the last couple of days.

Did your good parent help you with this?

_____

What did you say to yourself?

_____

_____

Did you help yourself feel better?

_____

_____

Did you engage in problem-solving?

_____

_____

_____

What will you do to correct the problem?

_____

_____

_____

_____

Conclusion

You can see that being your own good parent/guide is the most important thing you can do for yourself. It is what will propel you towards your goals and dreams.

CHAPTER 7

Enlist Needed Help: You Are Not Alone

Introduction: We all need help!

In the last chapter, we looked at how you become your own guide in life, responsible and independent. In this chapter, we look at how you get the help you need. These two things are not opposites. Everyone needs help sometimes. Being independent doesn't mean going it alone; it means making decisions that keep your goals in mind and serve you the best.

So, let's look at why would teens and young adults need help:

Choose the best answer:

They're young and lack experience

They don't know their way around

School subjects are difficult

They're not ready to be on their own

All of these are true

Part 1. What Kind of Help Do You Need?

Are you at grade level in reading? In math? These are the most important subjects. How to get to grade level if you are not there? Tutors in the community? Special programs in schools? Self-help online? You can do this. Your future depends on it. What help do you need?

a. _____

b. _____

c. _____

d. _____

It's most important to get help with school subjects while at school. Do you ask questions in class? Do you go to before-school or after-school tutorials? Do you go to special classes for some subjects? What will you do to get help? Remember that this is for you, not for anyone else. You're entitled to the best life you can get. How will you work towards it?

a. _____

_____

_____

b. _____

_____

_____

c. _____

_____

_____

Help with homework, at home, or outside of school? Do you ask family members? Do you look up your school subjects online? Do you use Khan Academy or YouTube videos to get lessons explained? What will you do to help yourself to a big serving of that success pie?

a. _____

_____

_____

b. _____

_____

_____

c. _____

_____

_____

d. _____

_____

_____

It is hard now, but it gets easier as you learn to take care of yourself. You need to learn to get help even when the challenges are great. Teens must learn that challenges are everywhere, but you have already learned to meet challenges. Remember learning to walk, to talk, to use the toilet, to read, to write, to count, to ride a bicycle, to play on a team? Now is the time for the new challenges in your life.

Part 2. How Do You Find Help in Your Community?

    a. Do you ask your parents?

    b. Do you ask your school counselor?

    c. Do you ask your grade advisor?

    d. Does your school have an online resource for community programs?

    e. Do you look online on your own?

    f. Do you ask at church or at the Y?

It is of course "all of the above." Do your best to be a detective and ask around, find out what the options are. The more you have in your information basket, the better off you can be.

Part 3. Your Challenges

What if you have a disability such as ADHD, Learning Disabilities, or an even more challenging emotional or physical situation? All schools provide special help for those situations, sometimes, in a regular classroom, sometimes, in a separate classroom, or another school campus. It is important to accept this help even if it embarrasses you, makes you feel different. The truth is that it allows you to have just as good a chance at a good future as those who don't struggle with those challenges.

What are your personal challenges?

    1. _____

       _____

    2. _____

       _____

    3. _____

       _____

Are you getting the help you need? What could you do if you felt you needed more help?

a. Talk to the school counselor

b. Talk to your parents

c. Talk to the Assistant Principal or Principal

d. Talk to your teachers

What will you do?

_____

_____

What will you say? Can you be as specific in your needs as possible?

Need # 1 _____

Need # 2 _____

Need # 3 _____

Do you have other needs? It is important to know what you need so that you can ask for help.

Need # 4 _____

Need # 5 _____

Part 4. Challenges at Home: Obstacles to Your School Performance

a. Are you able to do homework at home?

b. Do you have a place to do it, undisturbed?

c. Do you have responsibilities that get in the way?

d. Do you have a job?

e. Do you have to watch siblings?

f. Do you have to do a lot of housework?

What is your situation?

_____

_____

_____

Part 5. Severe Problems at Home: a Difficult Challenge

    a.   There is only one parent or caretaker.

    b.   Parents or caretakers are out of work.

    c.   There are too many people in the home.

    d.   There are drugs and alcohol being used.

    e.   No adult is there to watch children.

    f.   Children are being abused, verbally, emotionally, physically, or sexually.

How is your situation at home? How do you get help when your situation is exceedingly difficult? It can be very scary to ask for help. How do you get the courage to reach out?

Who can you reach out to if you are living in exceedingly difficult conditions that are not good or safe for you?

    a.   Siblings that live outside the home

    b.   Other relatives outside your home

    c.   Teachers at school will send you to a counselor

    d.   Counselors at school must help (it's the law)

    e.   Psychologists can help with getting protection

    f.   A religious organization

    g.   Child Protective Services

    h.   The police for immediate help

It is very scary to call on Child Protective Services, but they can really help. You may have to be under their protection for a while. When you make the decision to get better care, you're helping yourself and your whole family. If you have siblings, you're helping them, and you are also helping the adults to make a better home for their children. Sometimes, home doesn't get better and you need to live with a foster family for a while. Foster families can be lifesavers.

Part 6. Help for Young Adults

Once you leave home, the problems and challenges become different. Maybe you're attending college and are having a hard time. Maybe you already have a job and it is challenging. Some young adults have families and responsibilities for children. Others are still looking to find their way, unemployed and often engaging in risky behaviors.

There is, of course, help for all these situations and others, too. There is always help everywhere and it is your responsibility to get it.

1. Help when you are attending college. How will you seek the help you need?

    a. Remedial courses help you improve your skills.

    b. Counseling centers provide support when you are feeling distressed.

    c. Career counseling helps identify career choices.

    d. There may be help with job placement or available campus jobs.

    e. Dorms have house parents for advice.

    f. Faculty have office hours to discuss your situation and your work.

    g. Other: _____

2. Help with problems at work. What help do you need now? How will you find it?

    a. Human Resources departments help with information about benefits.

    b. Human Resources departments help with your rights as an employee when there are conflicts between employees or with a supervisor.

    c. You can join a union that protects workers' rights.

    d. Your State has laws to protect employees – information with phone numbers to call is posted for all to access.

    e. Other: _____

3. Help when you are not employed or going to school in your young adult years. Maybe you're still at home or living with others, searching for your path forward. That's often when you need the most help.

Help with mental health:

a. Seek counseling from public or private sources.

b. Seek help with addiction from public hospitals or programs.

Help with disabilities:

a. Public and private agencies have resources to help. You can find help online for specific disabilities.

b. Sheltered workshops may be a resource at this time. These provide help for persons not able to hold regular jobs.

Help with employment:

a. Work force or employment centers help you find jobs.

b. State sponsored training is often available. Look for information online or contact your state offices.

c. US Armed Forces may be a good job opportunity; they offer great benefits.

Help with getting into college:

a. Grants and scholarships are available. Your high school counselor can help with these. So can the college you choose.

b. You can qualify for educational loans. These are managed at the college you attend.

c. Help with preparing for the GED. Courses are available online or at many high schools.

d. Help is available to Veterans; get information from the Veterans' Administration.

e. Colleges offer remedial courses to help students catch up with their skills. This helps them succeed in college.

f. Online courses are available in many areas, either for general knowledge or towards a college degree. Many colleges have advisors to help you plan your work.

4. Please take the time to identify your situation and your needs. Then choose possible ways to get help.

a. Need # 1

_____

Help needed from:

_____

_____

_____

b. Need # 2

_____

Help needed from:

_____

_____

_____

c. Need # 3

_____

Help needed from:

_____

_____

_____

_____

d. Need # 4

_____

Help needed from:

_____

_____

_____

Part 7. Help for Difficulties with the Law

Many young people have gotten in trouble with the law and it is difficult for them to figure out how to get their life back on track. If you are on probation, parole, or incarcerated, it is essential for you to accept any help you can get.

1. There are treatment programs. If you are mandated to get treatment, do your best to overcome your difficulties and remember your dreams. It is okay to dream even if you have made mistakes. Mistakes don't doom you. Don't give up on yourself.

2. There are programs for rehabilitation. Some people have made themselves careers even when they were in prison. It is essential to realize your own goodness, become your own good parent who will lead you out of a difficult situation. It is important to seek all the help you can get.

3. There are scholarships specifically for people who have been in prison and paid their debt to society.

4. There are places to help you find work.

There is no doubt that it is hard work, but it is necessary work if you want to have a good life.

It is never hopeless. It is never too late to take better care of yourself.

Conclusion:

The most important piece is to never give up. You deserve good treatment from others and sometimes, you must insist on it. It is difficult, but it helps you develop special strengths. I see so many people who have been through a very tough early life but have made good lives for themselves, despite that. (Why do they still need me then? I usually see people who struggle with their memories of the rough times and want to find peace).

CHAPTER 8

Identify Your Wishes: Follow Your Dreams

Introduction

In the last chapters, you've been learning how to manage yourself, your emotions, your behavior, your need for help. Now it's time to focus on your dreams. Everyone has dreams. Maybe only one, maybe several. Dreams are important. They are essential. They give you energy and direction. To reach your dreams and make then a reality, you need to set goals for yourself. Everyone is always reaching for a goal. Sometimes, it's a tiny, daily goal: getting your homework done, playing with friends, engaging in a sport, making a goal or a basket, getting your chores done.

But here we'll be learning about big dreams. Big dreams guide your life. Dreams give life meaning. Dreams are what we can't live without. Even if you feel that you don't have dreams, that life is just too tough and dreams don't come true anyway, somewhere deep within you, you have a dream. You may have hidden it carefully. You may be afraid that it's just a dream. It's impossible. It's never going to happen. Well, you can't be the judge of that. So, let yourself dream. And try to reach for that dream. Many people have succeeded despite exceedingly difficult odds. You won't know until you try.

If you want to succeed, you need to make your dream your guiding light, that which you are always striving for. You need to believe in your dream. Most people have doubts. That's normal. Still, they want to strive towards their dream. Having faith that your dream is right for you and working towards it is essential. Having faith in yourself and your strength to keep trying is essential.

Part I. Naming Your Dream

Did you have a dream when you were younger? What was it?

_____

_____

_____

Did you share it? How did others react?

_____

_____

_____

Were you encouraged? Were you discouraged? Were you made fun of or criticized?

_____

_____

_____

Were you told it could never happen? That it was impossible? Were you given reasons?

_____

_____

_____

This can stay with you as you grow up, particularly the negative voices.

It's important to bypass or overcome these voices if they were negative. They weren't yours. They belonged to others. Make sure to leave them behind, discard them.

How do you now recover your dream, decide if it is still your dream today?

Do you still have that dream or maybe another dream now?

_____

Does it fit you well?

_____

Is it worth working for?

_____

_____

Do you believe in yourself?

_____

_____

Do you have the courage to fight for this dream?

_____

_____

Dreams take work. What kind of work will your dream take?

_____

_____

Dreams take courage. What does that mean to you? How will you gather your courage?

_____

_____

Dreams take determination (sticking with it). What does that mean to you? How will you stick with your goals?

_____

_____

Dreams take perseverance (keeping going). What does that mean to you? How will you keep going even when there are setbacks?

_____

_____

Part 2. Making Your Dream Real

You are standing at a crossroads and trying to decide where to go. There are many signs to different places. How will you choose? You need to know where you want to go. You need to know the path there, at least somewhat, so that you don't go in the wrong direction.

Well, life is just like that. We need to know where we want to go, and we need to have an idea of how to get there. When we are in our teen years, we have dreams for ourselves. Maybe we are hiding them. Maybe we think they're just not real, not for us. Maybe, we have them squarely in front of us.

That is the best. It may be a grand dream that you know is going to be tough to reach. It may be a dream your parents have for you and you think it will fit you. It may be that you want to follow the leadership of someone you really admire, follow their dream too. It may remain just a dream for right now because you don't dare yet to have goals for yourself.

* * *

You have a dream, or even many dreams, near and far, small and large, for your life. When we know where we want to go, we must find the path or paths to get there. How do we learn about those? That is our responsibility. We often share our dreams with others; we ask for help. Parents and caregivers help. Teachers help. School counselors help. People in the community help. The internet helps. There is so much information online…So, we can have an idea of our path to those goals.

Once we have a path, we need to identify the stepping-stones along that path. Stepping-stones can be large at first; then they get broken down into small steps.

Exercise 1: Order the following steps required to become a doctor: this is one of the longest paths.

    a. Go to medical school

    b. Take pre-med courses in college

    c. Take college entrance exam

    d. Pass board examination

    e. Get an internship

    f. Do well in math and science in high school

    g. Take medical school entrance exam

    h. Graduate from high school

    i. Get specialty residency experience

Exercise 2: Order the steps required to become a baker:

    a. Get internship in a bakery during the summer

    b. Do well in high school

    c. Graduate high school

    d. Go to cooking school

    e. Become an apprentice to a baker

    f. Volunteer to help in a bakery

Exercise 3: Order the steps required to become a teacher:

    a. Take college entrance exam

    b. Do two years of student teaching

    c. Do well in high school

    d. Graduate college

    e. Get teaching license

    f. Graduate high school

    g. In college, concentrate on subject you want to teach.

    h. Take education skills courses in college

Exercise 4: Order the steps required to become an auto mechanic:

    a. Get summer jobs in a garage or auto repair shop

    b. Go to mechanic school to become an expert mechanic

    c. Get a HS diploma or GED

    d. Volunteer to help in an auto repair shop

Part 3. Set Goals for Yourself

Do you know what goals lay in front of you? Do you know what the stepping-stones are? Are you paying attention to them? Where are you on the path? How do you make sure to stay on the path?

Exercise: Name your biggest dream for yourself:

_____

_____

What goals must you meet to get there? Please list them in order.

a. _____

b. _____

c. _____

d. _____

e. _____

Where are you on that path?

_____

_____

_____

What's next for you?

_____

_____

_____

Be patient with yourself. Dreams are often a lifetime endeavor. You're just at the very beginning. Sometimes there are lots of steps to get to your goal. Sometimes you must change your path along the way. Determination and perseverance make dreams happen. Without them, dreams remain dreams. Remember that it's never too late to make a dream happen.

Part 4. Staying on Your Path Takes Effort Every Day

There are lots of stepping-stones leading to the main goals.

Lots of adults like to make lists of everyday goals to keep track of them. It's so easy to get distracted and forget things. You've already seen lists of steps to everyday goals in Chapter 3. This is like that.

On the next pages you will have the chance to practice listing your goals for the day and then for the week. You might want to do lists for months or even semesters, listing assignments and projects. Looking at the list and seeing what you accomplish is enjoyable and can help you stay on track.

Don't forget to praise yourself for what you accomplish even if you didn't finish all the items on the list. You might even like to keep the lists to track what you have accomplished.

Don't forget to go back to the Identity Scale and check on your progress: how are you meeting your personal goals? How do you feel about yourself? It is always good to check in with yourself.

My Daily Goals Example	Your Goals for Today
1. Have breakfast	1. ....
2. Take a shower	2. ....
3. Shampoo my hair	3. ....
4. Treat my hair	4. ....
5. Work on Chapter 7	5. ....
6. Work on book format	6. ....
7. Have lunch	7. ....
8. Watch news program	8. ....
9. Prepare dish for potluck	9. ....
10. Drive to potluck	10. ....
11. Rent a car for upcoming trip	11. ....
12. Call bank about missing mileage	12. ....
13. Check weather for trip	13. ....
14. Prepare for Monday's business call	14. ....
15.	15. ....
16.	16. ....
17.	17. ....
18.	18. ....
19.	19. ....
20.	20. ....

Your Goals for the Next Week

1. ....
2. ....
3. ....
4. ....
5. ....
6. ....
7. ....
8. ....
9. ....
10. ....
11. ....
12. ....
13. ....
14. ....
15. ....
16. ....
17. ....
18. ....
19. ....
20. ....

Your Goals for the Week After

1. ....
2. ....
3. ....
4. ....
5. ....
6. ....
7. ....
8. ....
9. ....
10. ....
11. ....
12. ....
13. ....
14. ....
15. ....
16. ....
17. ....
18. ....
19. ....
20. ....

Your Goals for the Next Month

1. ....
2. ....
3. ....
4. ....
5. ....
6. ....
7. ....
8. ....
9. ....
10. ....
11. ....
12. ....
13. ....
14. ....
15. ....
16. ....
17. ....
18. ....
19. ....
20. ....

Your Goals for the Semester

1. ....
2. ....
3. ....
4. ....
5. ....
6. ....
7. ....
8. ....
9. ....
10. ....
11. ....
12. ....
13. ....
14. ....
15. ....
16. ....
17. ....
18. ....
19. ....
20. ....

Part 5. Your Dreams Are Your Private Property

No one can take them from you. People can try to discourage you. People will compete with you. People may try to sabotage you because they are jealous of your determination. You may have to fight for your dream. This is very usual; it's not easy. A great dream is worth fighting for. A great dream is worth overcoming all obstacles.

My examples of being sabotaged in meeting my goals:

a. Once, when I was about 12, I was bringing my successful science project to school. A classmate asked to see it and I showed it to her. She did her best to destroy my experiment (I had collected a mushroom's spores and they made a beautiful pattern on cardboard). Fortunately, she didn't succeed but I was upset at her meanness.

b. My sister always had "an emergency" when I was trying to study for a test. I had to help her out. She knew that I wouldn't say "no."

c. My ex-husband always skipped his turn to have the kids when I had an important exam the next week (I was studying to become a psychologist). I finally learned not to let him know about my stepping stones.

d. In college, I had a teacher who had seemed to like me, but then gave me a very unjustified bad grade for the term. He wouldn't change it. I didn't appeal it because I was too shy.

e. Another time, I had trusted a professor with my frustration with an assignment where I could not find the materials needed. He later went out of his way to ask me about that assignment and failed me for not doing it. I was again too shy to fight and I have regretted it for a long time.

Now, it's your turn to look at your experiences.

Has someone made fun of your goal?

_____

_____

Has someone tried to discourage you from your goal?

_____

_____

Has someone tried to sabotage what you were doing?

_____

_____

What have you learned from these experiences?

_____

_____

Can you protect yourself more effectively now?

_____

_____

It is important to own your dreams and do your best to protect them from those who want you ill. It is also important to fight for your rights and your dreams. Being too afraid to do it leads to great regrets.

Part 6. How Are You Doing with Your Dream?

This is a good place to journal. You can write about your own experience. Are you working towards making your dream come true? Remember it can be a tiny dream as well as a large dream. If you have no dream at all, you may want to explore how you feel about having dreams.

If you have a dream, are you able to focus on your goals? How is it going for you? What's going well? What's a big challenge? Are there problems? How could you solve them?

Remember: this is a private space for you to explore what is important to you.

_____

_____

_____

_____

_____

_____

_____

_____

CHAPTER 9

Keep Moving Towards Your Goals: Avoid Being Distracted

Introduction

There are many things that can get in the way of moving towards our goals.

Some obstacles are inside us. We'll start with looking at what we need to do to overcome inner blocks to our success. Many obstacles are outside of us and we need to learn to navigate them.

You will recognize parts from Chapter 3. I am posting them here again for two reasons:

1. It is most important to know yourself and to understand what helps you move forward, as well as what keeps you stuck and frustrated.

2. Things may have changed for you. You already conquered some of the fears mentioned earlier and want to face some other fears.

Part 1. When Fear Gets in the Way

What might make you move away from your dreams for yourself? Even those teens that believe they have no dreams do have dreams which are often buried deep inside of them. Some obsta-cles are inside us and we'll start by looking at what you need to do to overcome inner blocks to your success.

A lot of the time, it is your fear and your anger that rob you of having dreams and pursuing them. It is most important for you to know your fears and anger.

When fear is guiding you. It is important to face your fears and find ways to move forward. Let's look at the common fears that get in the way.

We need to become more courageous. COURAGEOUS means that we challenge and overcome our fears, not that they disappear.

Starting with little steps. To build up your courage, you need to:

1. Acknowledge your fear, face your fear, and work to get past it. Being courageous doesn't mean having no fear, it means doing things despite the fear.

2. Always start with the easiest thing to build up your confidence. Remember there is no magic, but you can do the work of becoming who you want to be.

Exercise 1: My first fear to overcome is: _____

_____

What can I do to challenge it and conquer it?

_____

_____

Did I do that?

_____

_____

Did I succeed in doing it? (If not, don't give up. Try another approach).

_____

_____

How did I feel after that?

_____

_____

You can go back to the Identity Scale and see if you want to move the button for that quality.

Exercise 2: My next fear to overcome is:

_____

_____

What can I do to challenge it and conquer it?

_____

_____

Did I do that?

_____

_____

Did I succeed in doing it? (Again, if you didn't succeed, you can try different things).

_____

_____

How did I feel after that?

_____

_____

You can go back to the Identity Scale and see if you want to move the marker for that quality.

Part 2. When Anger Gets in the Way

Sometimes, it's anger that gets in the way of accomplishing our goals. Anger is important. It is our reaction to fear and pain. Looking at our anger often takes us back to our fear and to what hurts us.

Anger is often accompanied by despair and giving up. So, it is essential to know and understand our anger and then figure out how to use that energy to get us past the anger. (More in Chapter 9).

Begin by figuring out the source of your anger. What are you angry about? Are you angry with your school experience? Are you angry with parents or caregivers? Your home situation? Are you angry with the way society treats you? Angry with the way the world treats you? Are you angry with God?

Let's take them one at a time. Maybe you can figure out how to manage.

Exercise 1: Angry at school? Angry with schoolmates? Why?

You're being bullied. What can you do?

Would you report it to teachers?

_____

Would you ignore the bully? Walk away?

_____

Do you want to fight the bullies?

_____

Can you take care of yourself (self-soothing) and move on?

_____

Can you keep your goal in mind?

_____

You feel that you can't succeed at school.

Do you compare yourself to others? Does it help?

_____

Could you work harder? Get the help you need?

_____

Do you want to do better? Would you make it happen?

_____

Can you keep your goal in mind, keep moving forward?

_____

Others are more popular than you are.

Are you usually friendly with others?

_____

Are you a good friend?

_____

Are you a leader or a follower? Or even a loner?

_____

Can you look at your qualities on the Identity Scale?

_____

Can you see what you need to improve?

_____

Exercise 2: Angry with parents/caregivers? Start by identifying why they make you angry.

Do they treat you well?

_____

_____

Are they fair?

_____

_____

Are they kind?

_____

_____

Are they helpful?

_____

_____

Do they take care of you?

_____

_____

Do they provide a good home?

_____

_____

Do you feel safe at home?

_____

_____

Is there enough food for everyone?

_____

_____

Do you have a place to sleep? Do your homework?

_____

_____

What are your responsibilities at home?

_____

_____

_____

Too many chores, assignments?

_____

_____

Not enough chores, responsibilities?

_____

_____

Are there large problems at home?

_____

_____

When there are large problems at home, problems you're having a hard time coping with, it is important to get help.

Start by identifying people you can get help from:

A trusted relative

A trusted neighbor

A counselor at school

A psychologist at school

A church leader or trusted person

Helpers in community shelters

Have the courage to get help from CPS

Exercise 3: Angry with society and the world. This is a real and difficult issue, one that needs adults to intervene. Unfortunately, it often takes a long time for change to come about.

Lots of people think that society is not fair, and it often is not.

Seeking justice, overcoming prejudice and racism is exceedingly difficult.

People are marching in the streets to demand more justice.

There are groups that can help.

You can steel yourself against injustice and keep moving ahead – every little step helps you reach your goal.

You can be determined to take your place in the world, helping others do it, too.

Exercise 4: Angry with God

People think it's not fair that they have such challenges.

Other people think God is testing them...that He wants them to be stronger. That's a better attitude. Respond to the challenges.

So many people have succeeded despite great challenges, or maybe because of them. They went full steam ahead, convinced of their power to overcome. We call them heroes, but everyone can be a hero.

They succeed because they do the work of finding their way forward.

Part 3. Managing Interactions With Others

Obstacles that you may encounter every day as you interact with other people.

Do you know how to safeguard your dream?

Do you know how to avoid the distractions that will throw you off your path?

Do you know how to choose friends who encourage you to reach your goals?

Do you know how to avoid people who discourage you or interfere with your reaching your goals?

Do you know how to choose romantic partners that respect and encourage you?

Do you know how to avoid romantic partners that only want you to please them?

Do you know how to avoid romantic partners that will interfere or discourage you from your goals?

Do you have friends who need a lot of help from you, help that often needs to come from adults?

Do you know how to encourage and help your friends get help from adults?

All those questions are important: they might make the difference between reaching your goals and not reaching your goals.

Exercise 1: Look carefully at the examples of behavior below and mark them as Helpful (+) or Not Helpful (-), at the left of the examples.

a. Your best friend wants to study with you.

b. Your new friend wants to smoke weed with you after school.

c. A classmate wants you to skip class with him and go hang out.

d. Your new friend dares you to go fight the bully after school.

e. A classmate wants to buy your notes and then cheat off you on the test.

f. Your new romantic interest wants you to party instead of studying for a test.

g. Your friends are encouraging you to skip work and go to the mall.

h. Your good friend dares you to go shoplifting at the discount store.

i. Your friend offers to lend you some interesting books about your dream goal.

j. A former friend is angry and spreads rumors about you.

k. A new group of friends wants to form a study group for a big test.

l. A close friend has problems at home and needs you to help her.

m. A close friend has secrets that she wants you to keep from her parents.

Exercise 2: Which of the above examples have you experienced? How did you handle them? What were the consequences to you?

a. _____

_____

_____

b. _____

_____

_____

c. _____

_____

_____

d. _____

_____

_____

e. _____

_____

_____

Part 4. Looking Inside Again

Are there behaviors that you do that promote or interfere with your own goals? Behaviors that promote or interfere with your friends' goals? Are you a good friend to your friends? This is an important part of finding good friends and romantic partners.

Exercise 1: List things that you do that move YOU towards your goal, and behaviors that move you away from your goal:

a. towards

_____

_____

b. towards

_____

_____

c. towards

_____

_____

d. away

_____

_____

e. away

_____

_____

f. away

_____

_____

Exercise 2: List things that you do that promote your friends' goals, and behaviors that interfere with their goals:

a. Promote

_____

_____

b. Promote

_____

_____

c. Promote

_____

_____

d. Interfere

_____

_____

e. Interfere

_____

_____

f. Interfere

_____

_____

Part 5. Looking out for NUMBER ONE!

Maybe you've heard that saying. It sounds selfish, maybe even egotistical (a big word for self-centered), but in psychology, when it comes to your well-being, it is essential. Taking care of yourself is necessary. Only you know:

1. what you really want for yourself

2. what you need and when you need it

3. what feels good to you and what doesn't

4. what you don't want

5. what doesn't feel right for you

6. that only YOU can be happy with yourself

When you are taking care of your needs, doing the right things for yourself, then you are on top of your form.

Exercise 1: Name the first three needs you have right now:

1. _____

2. _____

3. _____

Exercise 2: Will you attend to them as best as you can? What will you do? How will it fit?

1. _____

_____

2. _____

_____

3. _____

_____

Part 6. Denying Your Needs is Harmful

When you are denying your needs, it does not feel right. It becomes difficult to make things work for you. You might lose sight of your goals for the day and get confused. That will be painful, and you will feel upset. You will harbor anger and resentment, maybe towards others you allowed to get in the way, or even towards yourself because you disappointed yourself.

Often, we need to have others like us and we do them favors that interfere with our goals. Unfortunately, that often does not help us feel more popular, nor does it really help them.

Exercise 1: Describe one example of when you put someone else's needs before yours and you felt that you cheated yourself:

_____

_____

_____

_____

Exercise 2: Now, share one example of when you disregarded your own need and then were frustrated with yourself? This can happen when we are trying to help a friend who is distressed and really needs adult help. You can lose track of your needs when the friend's needs are overwhelming. This happens to most of us until we learn to listen to our inner voice, to our needs. Has this happened to you?

One example might be:

You stayed up late last night talking with this person you really want to help. Then you felt tired this morning. Stayed in bed late, had to skip brushing your teeth and breakfast. Now, you are hungry and grouchy and certainly not your best self. Will you remember to be more focused on your needs next time? It is entirely up to you to be clear about your needs and limitations.

The truth is that this friend will benefit more if you show clear limits. That friend will respect you more as well and realize that they are responsible for getting the right help.

Maybe you have an example of a situation that you experienced:

_____

_____

_____

_____

_____

_____

_____

_____

CHAPTER 10

Kick Obstacles Out of Your Way and Maintain Your Momentum

Introduction

This chapter reviews many of the things you've been working on. It's a quick reminder of how to make good things happen for you.

How important is it to pursue your dreams? It must be one of the most important things in your life. Dreams are not easy to pursue; that's why they're called dreams. We are the only ones who can make them a reality. Only you can make your own dream a reality.

Pursuing a dream is a lot like practicing a sport. Maybe the sport is your dream. You must train. You must practice. You must be focused and avoid distraction. You must get the right mind set to succeed.

Part 1. Begin to Work Towards Your Goals

Exercise 1: Remember, you must defeat the fear. What negative voices do you hear? Can you add different ones?

 a. I'm not smart enough

 b. I can't do it

 c. No one will help me

 d. It is just too hard

 e. I can't afford college

 f. I won't succeed even if I try

 g. What's the use? Everything falls apart anyway

 h. _____

151

i. _____

j. _____

What will you do to get those negative voices out of your head and move forward?

Find your good voice, your good inner parent who encourages you, who wants the best for you, who helps you when you fall.

Exercise 2: Circle the ones you use to encourage yourself? What else do you tell yourself to keep going towards your dreams?

a. Everyone can have a dream

b. I can do it if I set my mind to it

c. I am as good as anyone else

d. I am entitled to the best life I can have

e. Only I can do this for myself

f. I won't give up

g. I have what it takes

h. It's never too late

i. _____

j. _____

k. _____

Part 2. Gather Your Courage

It's normal to be afraid. We are all afraid. After all, there is a lot at stake when you want to acknowledge and then strive for your dreams. Courage is pursuing your dreams despite your fear.

Exercise 1: It takes courage to succeed. What's the meaning of courage? Only one of these is correct: can you find it?

a. Fearlessness

b. Doing things despite the fear

c. Bragging about being fearless

d. Daring others to take big steps

e. Attempting things on a dare

Exercise 2: Remember that pursuing your dreams happens one step at a time, one day at a time.

f. It takes a small effort every day. What is your step today?

_____

_____

g. It takes a lot of days. What is your nearest goal? How many days will it take to get to your nearest goal?

_____

_____

h. What is your current goal? Remember that you have time. You have your whole life ahead of you to achieve your goals.

_____

_____

i. Things always get in the way. What got in the way yesterday?

_____

_____

j. Did you manage to stay on track? If not, how will you get back?

_____

_____

k. What problems are in the way today?

_____

_____

l. How will you handle them?

_____

_____

m. Be creative. You have the answers. How could you overcome each of these problems?

_____

_____

Exercise 3: Are there people getting in the way of your goals? Who are they? How do you confront them or get around them?

Name: _____

_____

_____

Name: _____

_____

_____

Name: _____

_____

Exercise 4: Will you remember to put yourself first? This is your dream and no one else can do this work for you?

What will you do to ensure that you put yourself first?

a. Listen to your voice that tells you what you need.

_____

_____

b. Avoid being misled by others.

_____

_____

c. Be careful about following advice. Use your judgement.

_____

_____

d. Avoid giving in to people who want you to do their bidding or take care of them.

_____

_____

e. Check in with yourself before offering help to others or doing things to please them.

_____

_____

Exercise 5: Will you make sure your friends respect you and treat you well?

f. Do you know how to make friends that are good for you?

_____

_____

g. Do you have friends that have your back?

_____

_____

h. Do your friends support you and your dreams?

_____

_____

Exercise 6: Remember that you're not alone.

There is help everywhere. It is your responsibility to find it and ask for it, as needed. No problem is too small or too large. Your dream is worth every effort.

a. What help do you need today?

_____

_____

b. Where will you get it?

_____

_____

c. Whom will you ask?

_____

_____

Exercise 7: How will you make sure that it is the help you need?

a. Were you understood correctly?

_____

_____

b. Can you check if the information is correct?

_____

_____

c. Do you still need more information?

_____

_____

Part 3. Your Dream is Most Important

Don't let anyone, not even yourself, talk you out of it. Remember that it is your dream and only you can make it happen. That is your responsibility. Remind yourself of your dream. How are you managing so far? Are you satisfied? Do you need to change something? Get better at something? Remember also that it is never too late. Even if you lose your path, you can always get back on it. Don't forget the saying; "where there is a will, there is a way." That's what it is about. Do not give up on your dream.

Exercise 1: What else could you do to get the courage to pursue your dream?

_____

_____

_____

Exercise 2: Can you think of something that you haven't done?

_____

_____

_____

Exercise 3: Is there something you need to get out of the way?

_____

_____

_____

Exercise 4: Is there some habit you need to change or acquire?

_____

_____

_____

Exercise 5: What else do you need to get on your path to your goal?

_____

_____

_____

Part 4: Room for Journaling

This is your life and you're choosing how you want to lead it. This is a space to put down your thoughts.

_____

_____

CHAPTER 11

Coping With Problems in Your Life, Your Family, Your Community

Winning at Life

For many teens and young adults, life is far from easy or simple. There are just too many things that are getting in the way. Many things getting in the way does not mean that it is impossible to succeed but it means it will be harder. But you need to know that you can cope with and overcome difficulties.

As a matter of fact, it has been discovered that young people who have had a hard early life are more resilient (stronger) and do better than those who have had it easy. These teens and young adults have learned how to meet challenges and win!

I have divided the many possible challenges into separate categories. Some have already been addressed in this workbook, some not. Again, this is meant to help you become more aware of your challenges and find ways to cope with them. There are many ways to cope positively; these help you towards success.

Part 1. Coping with Learning Disabilities

Many people have ADHD, Dyslexia, Learning Difficulties

Those make it harder to succeed in school

It's harder but not impossible

Schools have many ways of helping

You are owed the help – it is only fair

You may feel different and uncomfortable

You can learn to manage those feelings

You can certainly succeed

Exercise 1: Please state any learning disability you are experiencing and how it affects you:

a. _____
_____
_____

b. _____
_____
_____

c. _____
_____
_____

d. _____
_____
_____

Exercise 2: What do you do to overcome these obstacles?

a. _____
_____
_____

b. _____
_____
_____

c. _____
_____
_____

d. _____
_____
_____

Part 2. Many People Have Physical Disabilities

Many people have lifelong physical disabilities that keep them from seeing, hearing, walking, standing, having good muscle control

Large physical disabilities can slow you down

You need to learn to accept limitations

You need to work around them and learn different skills

You need to teach others to respect you

You need to teach others that you don't need pity

Exercise 1: Please name any physical disability you are experiencing and how it affects you:

a. _____

_____

_____

b. _____

_____

_____

c. _____

_____

_____

d. _____

_____

_____

Exercise 2: What do you do to cope with and overcome this disability?

a. _____

_____

_____

b. _____

_____

c. _____

_____

_____

d. _____

_____

_____

Part 3. Disabilities Due to Accidents or Illness Require Adaptation

People need to mourn their loss of function

People then need to adapt to their "new" reality

Sometimes, they need to learn to see themselves differently

This is extremely challenging even with rehabilitation

Exercise 1: Have you suffered an accident or illness? What happened?

_____

_____

_____

Exercise 2: How has it changed you? How do you cope? How do you overcome the problems?

_____

_____

_____

_____

Part 4. Difficulties Due to Traumatic Abuse or Neglect

Unfortunately, many children and teens suffer from abuse, in the home or from someone they know. Sometimes, it is from a stranger.

This is different from the previous situation and I believe it needs a category by itself.

First, let me remind you that there is help for children and teens who are being abused. It is not an acceptable situation. Unfortunately, abuse is often not visible to others and it is entirely up to you to seek help.

There is help at home, at school, from safe relatives, and in the community. You can call the police and get help. This is a very tough trauma even if you can get help and make it stop, because it has already happened.

Abuse of any kind leaves lasting psychological scars. It also often delays your development because you are busy coping with the abuse and not attending to your personal growth. Survivors of abuse often feel they haven't learned essential things and are now far behind others in school or social skills.

If you are unfortunate enough to have suffered abuse in the past, I want to invite you to write about it here. Of course, that is not enough, I also want you to have the courage to get help if you need it to recover.

IF YOU ARE SUFFERING ABUSE NOW, PLEASE GET HELP NOW!

What is the abuse that you have suffered?

_____

_____

_____

How has it affected you in your life?

_____

_____

_____

What do you do to cope with this wound, to overcome the pain and the shame? People often feel shame for having been abused. They feel it's their fault. IT'S NEVER YOUR FAULT.

_____

_____

_____

Were you able to get away from the abuse? What will you do if you are still being hurt? Will you get help? It's good to acknowledge and face up to it here, but it is NOT ENOUGH! Please get the help you need.

_____

_____

_____

It may be that you are already living in a foster or shelter situation. These situations take a lot of adaptation as well. Please write about what you encountered, what you learned, how you have adapted to a different situation.

_____

_____

_____

_____

_____

* * *

Part 5. Many Teens and Young Adults Have Emotional Difficulties

These are quite common and make life difficult. They are often caused by experiencing difficulties in the home. Many young people are depressed or anxious. Their environment is stressful and uncomfortable; they feel disempowered. Many are angry and vengeful when they feel they've been neglected or abused by parents or caretakers.

Please circle any item listed below that applies to you:

AFRAID   SAD   DEPRESSED   STRESSED   ANGRY   RAGING

LONELY   WANTING TO HURT OTHERS   WANTING TO BULLY OTHERS

ANXIOUS   WORRIED ALL THE TIME   WANTING TO HURT YOURSELF

SHY   AFRAID OF PEOPLE   WANTING TO END YOUR LIFE

FEELING DIFFERENT FROM OTHERS   FEELING YOU DON'T BELONG   FEARFUL

FEELING LIKE YOU'RE CRAZY   NOT FEELING LIKE YOURSELF AT TIMES

It is important to acknowledge when you are depressed or deeply disturbed and it is essential to get help. When you are angry and acting out, people will notice, and they will encourage you to get the help you need. This doesn't mean that you are wrong to be angry or that the problem is with you. Sometimes, youths need help using that energy positively to make the difference they want to see and not become self-destructive.

All these feelings are painful, and you need professional help. When you are depressed or anxious, it is not visible to others. Therefore, it is important to tell adults that you need help. Who can you talk to? Maybe it's your parent, a relative, your guardian, your cousin or aunt/uncle, your teacher, your counselor, you clergy person, or even a neighbor can be the one who helps you get help. It is not enough to talk to your friends. Even if they are supportive, they just cannot get you the help you need. Only an adult can help you here. Maybe you can get a friend to go with you and help you talk to an adult.

Part 6. Addiction to Alcohol or Drugs is a Significant Disability

Sometimes because of the above difficulties, many teens and young adults try to feel better by using alcohol and drugs. Some drugs are milder than others, but they all slow you down, distract you from your dreams and goals.

You may have given up on your dreams and goals…and are seeking refuge from the terrible feelings of loss and self-betrayal. That refuge is often using drugs and alcohol. Adults do it, too.

It is a sad time for you. It is an awful alternative to pursuing your goals. Nothing else gives you the energy and hope that you get from taking care of yourself and your life.

I hope you will realize that and turn yourself around. It is never too late.

Exercise 1: Have you had that experience? Have you started using drugs or alcohol when you felt discouraged, or sad, or depressed, or hopeless?

_____

_____

_____

Exercise 2: Did you find that drugs and alcohol helped you feel better? Maybe for a moment. Did you realize that they really don't help?

_____

_____

_____

Exercise 3: Have you been able, or will you be able to let go of addiction and then return to your life, take the helm of your lifeboat and steer it towards success?

_____

_____

_____

✶ ✶ ✶

Part 7. Limitations When You are in Trouble with the Law

This makes life particularly difficult. If you are lucky enough to be on probation, it is essential to do everything you can to get yourself in a better place. Accept the counseling. Accept any help to get you back on the path of fulfilling your dreams. Yes, you can have dreams. It is never too late to get on a good path to success.

If you have been convicted of a felony or have done time in jail/prison, it becomes more difficult to find work. Again, take advantage of any rehabilitation help you can find. You, too, can get back on a good path and work towards your goals. Many have done that and succeeded. You can, too!

Spending time in prison or even in a detention center is very unpleasant. Still, if you are incarcerated, it is a great opportunity to learn skills for after your release, to get counseling and encouragement to help you live a good life after leaving jail. Maybe, you'll remember your dreams and prepare yourself for your release: you'll make decisions that work for you. You'll realize that it's never too late to succeed.

There is a lot of concern right now about the justice system keeping people in prison way too long, how they make it nearly impossible to get out, even for small offenses. This is true for many people right now, but there is great energy to change this unfair system that does not look to rehabilitate prisoners. Many are hopeful that it will happen shortly. Be the first to take advantage of the change when it does happen, so that you can still enjoy a good life. It is never too late!

Part 8. Difficult Families Make it Difficult to Manage

There might be issues of divorce, of separation, of parents and caretakers coming and going, or your having to live in different places.

Exercise 1: Please share if this is something you are coping with:

_____

_____

_____

Exercise 2: What tools do you use for self-soothing? How do you take care of yourself?

_____

_____

_____

Exercise 3: What problems are you having with overcoming these obstacles?

_____

_____

_____

Part 9. When there is Illness or Unemployment in Your Home

These create a lot of stress and worry for the whole family. There might not be enough money for food or basic needs. You might be worried about the future. You might have to take on more tasks. You might even have to leave school to go to work to help support your family.

Exercise 1: Please share if this is something you are coping with:

_____

_____

_____

Exercise 2: What tools to you use for self-soothing? How do you take care of yourself?

_____

_____

_____

Exercise 3: How are you managing this difficult situation? What problems are you having with managing these challenges?

_____

_____

_____

* * *

Part 10. When Family Members are Using Drugs or Abusing Alcohol

This creates a difficult and unpleasant environment. Your parents may be unavailable and neglecting you and your siblings.

Exercise 1: Please share if this is something you are coping with:

_____

_____

_____

Exercise 2: What tools do you use for self-soothing? How do you take care of yourself?

_____

_____

_____

Exercise 3: What problems are you having with overcoming these challenges?

_____

_____

_____

Part 11. When there are Criminal Activities in the Home

This creates stress and danger for everyone. Some teens are invited to participate in those activities. Sometimes, teens get involved in crime.

If this is your situation, you have great decisions to make about your own life. Sometimes, teens can choose to go live with other relatives. Some teens run away. This is extremely dangerous; it is better to ask for help.

Exercise 1: Please share if this is something you are coping with:

_____

_____

_____

Exercise 2: How do you take care of yourself?

_____

_____

_____

Exercise 3: What decisions are you having to make?

_____

_____

_____

Part 12. Poverty is the Biggest and Most Common Obstacle

This often accompanies the above situations in your family. Often, it is a cause of these situations. People are desperate, live in poor conditions, don't have enough income to manage, and can't afford medical care. So, there is unemployment, illness, drug and alcohol abuse, and crime in the home.

But even this can be overcome as many successful persons who came from poor backgrounds show (you can go back to examples in the book).

If this is your situation, know that the best you can do for yourself and your family is to succeed and get out of poverty. Once you are successful, you might be able to help them improve their situation as well.

Exercise 1: Please share if this is something you are coping with:

_____

_____

_____

Exercise 2: What tools do you use for self-soothing? How do you take care of yourself?

_____

_____

_____

Exercise 3: What problems are you having with managing these challenges?

_____

_____

_____

Exercise 4: What kind of decisions are you making about your future? Are you getting the help that you need?

_____

_____

_____

Part 13. Remember that You are Entitled to Your Dreams

It is most important to come back to them again, even if you have given up on them a long time ago. Don't forget that those who overcome hardships and great challenges are the stronger for them. They're often more successful than those who have had it easy.

Identify your dreams and keep them squarely in front of you.

Be careful not to make them too small

Don't let others tell you that you can't do anything

Where there is a will, there is a way

Don't be the one who gives up on their dreams

Remember that coping with difficulties early on:

Makes you stronger

Can help you build good coping skills

Can help you be more creative

Gains you respect from others

This is the best training for success.

You can become a leader in your community

You can be popular

Strong people always attract others

You can inspire others to strive for their dreams

You have now completed the Workbook!

Congratulations!

You have read the Guidebook! You have done many or maybe all the exercises in this Workbook! Working the exercises, using the scales, and engaging with the decision trees, you have grown a lot of new skills!

You now feel more aware of yourself and the way you are with others and you're more aware of the choices that you make and how they impact your life. You feel your strengths when facing the small and large obstacles you encounter. You have goals you want to pursue and you are placing them squarely in front of you.

I hope you are pleased with yourself and with what you have accomplished. The tools remain yours to come back to at any time. They could be very useful when making decisions or confronting obstacles caused by others or circumstances. The scales can help you keep track of your progress.

Your life will feel difficult and challenging at times. Life is like that for most of us. I encourage you to never give up. Keep your dreams and goals alive. They will give you strength and courage; they will guide you throughout your life.

Thank you for the opportunity to help you along your path and I wish you the very best in life.

Acknowledgments

A great thank you to Marc Sawaya (Creative Consultant at RCCreative) for his ongoing support these many years and great artistry in adorning these books. Grateful for Corinne Marguerite Martch for her help in designing and composing the Sample Lists.

I want to express my deep appreciation to Raphael Sher for offering to edit this manuscript and rendering it more focused and eloquent. Many, many thanks to Rachel Badre, LPC, and Lisa Moss, for agreeing to be Beta readers. Their contributions have been priceless.

Many thanks to two young persons who agreed to be interviewed to ascertain that I was on the right track to speak to their needs. Much gratitude to my many young patients and students who helped me formulate this workbook to promote their path to success.

Much gratitude for my friend Franck Vermet's encouragement and his showing me that my idea could become a reality: an app to allow readers to keep track of their improvement in well-being, behavior, and decision making.

Many thanks to Ms. Oksana Yazeva, Free-Lance Programmer, who built the app to make my vision for self-evaluation, using the Identity and Behavior Scales, and for decision-making with Decision Trees, a reality.

Grateful for my many FB friends who provided ongoing encouragement and support.

Unending appreciation for my family and friends who have respected my time as I all too frequently eschewed invitations and commitments to leave room for writing.

I am also grateful to my many patients who have shown me that the Guidebook has helped them; I believe this companion Workbook will be equally useful, helping readers manage their lives with more purpose and satisfaction.